# THE SOUL OF A MAN

# THE SOUL OF A MAN

# DAVID HELLER

BALLANTINE BOOKS · NEW YORK

Grateful acknowledgment is made to Tyndale House Publishers, Inc.
for permission to reprint Scripture verses from *The Living Bible*.
Copyright © 1971. Used by permission of Tyndale House Publishers,
Inc., Wheaton, IL 60189. All rights reserved.

Library of Congress Cataloging-in-Publication Data

Heller, David.
The soul of a man / David Heller.—1st ed.
p.   cm.
Includes bibliographical references.
ISBN 0–345–36018–4
1. Men—Religious life.   2. Men (Psychology)   3. Men (Christian
theology)   I. Title
BV4843.H38   1990
248.8′42—dc20                                    90–31366
                                                      CIP

Design by Holly Johnson

Manufactured in the United States of America

First Edition: September 1990
10 9 8 7 6 5 4 3 2 1

*For my dearest Elizabeth,*
*whose loving presence is a gift*
*of divine origin.*
*From our first meeting at 7-Eleven,*
*to our engagement and marriage at Plymouth Rock,*
*our souls have met as one.*

# CONTENTS

# PREFACE

# WHAT IS A MAN?

I f being spiritual and believing in God is sissified, then count me among the biggest softies," asserted John, a thirty-three-year-old history teacher. With that succinct comment, John summarized his ideas about manhood along with his personal religious beliefs. For John, a man of discernible vision, a separation of maleness and godliness makes no sense. "If I am not being all that I can be," John continued, "if I am not all of me when I'm teaching or with my family, then I am cheating myself, and depriving myself of my God-given right to be a whole man."

John spoke frankly and eloquently concerning a subject that is shunned by too many men and women: the male soul. It is a great unspoken topic. In an era when women are changing by leaps and bounds, and exploration of their spiritual side is more commonplace, men have been strangely silent about their inner religious life. We have grown accustomed to the tiresome debate between the macho man and the intellectual man, but that polarity has not moved us ahead. It will not. For men have far greater depth, and far richer and more complex spiritual dimensions, than these simplistic stereotypes allow. Let it be appreciated by all of us: men and women have equal right to their souls and equal ability to develop spirituality.

I have explored the inner world of men because of the events and epiphanies in my own life. My struggle to become a true man has not been an easy one. In the process of growing up, I have had many lonely and empty nights. At times long periods of self-doubt and ample skepticism about the fairness of the world haunted me. I have hated and felt destructive feelings, sometimes at the same moment that I have loved and protected another person. The battles fought in my soul have raged on for years. Yet in the midst of my conflicts, in the eye of the storm, I have become more familiar with God. I know what it means to meet God. But that meeting does not take place outside of my male psyche or in some distant place, but wholly within the contours of my own manhood and my search for peace.

*The Soul of a Man* chronicles what I have discovered about God and man. Writing from personal experiences that opened my eyes to God's presence, and from intimate interviews with a variety of men, I shall picture the masculine soul as yearning for self-understanding, happiness, and a closer relationship to God. I explored the religious aspirations and crises of real men, rather than esoteric theories and studies, to paint my portrait of man.

I hope my book will help you in your own appreciation of men and God. I present principles of manhood, tools for

finding yourself and climbing higher spiritually. If you believe that you are more than a performance record or a
paycheck, then this book is written for you.

What are the challenges that confront us as men? To
answer that question, we must first understand our turbulent
times. We have witnessed great upheaval over the last thirty
years. The Vietnam War, the Watergate scandal, and the
Iran-Contra debacle—illustrations of failed foreign policy
and misguided leadership—have left us with a vacuum of
confidence in male authority. The sexual revolution changed
the way we think about morality and masculinity and cast into
open question our religious beliefs about sexuality. In addition, the women's movement of the seventies and eighties
and the emergence of increasing numbers of women in the
work force have dramatically shifted the relation between
the genders and altered domestic life. Even as we enter the
1990s we are still responding as men to the overwhelming
effects of the past three decades.

Because of these historical changes, the age-old question
"What is a man?" has once again become an acceptable and
even common question. At the same time that extremes in
masculine behavior reassert themselves and reactionary attitudes live on in some circles, many men are taking the more
moderate path of introspection. As our minds and hearts
respond to change, spiritual awakening is made possible and
the question of manhood can be fully answered.

To define himself and react to changes in society, a man
must first recognize he has a soul.

The soul is that dimension of a man which links him to
God and reveals eternal wisdom to him. I believe that it's by
design, and not coincidence, that a man's soul offers him
guidance for life. From the depths of his soul, a man uncovers

his unique purpose and the strength to achieve that purpose. The soul is the home of God's light and the crucial foundation upon which a man builds his life, though he may freely choose to follow his soul's teachings or depart from it. Making peace with our mothers and fathers and dealing with any childhood notions of manhood help us to build solid personal foundations and develop our souls. We must cultivate honesty while weeding out falsehood. We must learn the crucial difference between outward displays of bravado and genuine instances of courage. We must be willing to embrace a wide range of passions and experiences, free of fear, and make ready for a sense of personal faith in God.

We also define manhood by the everyday way we live our lives. Our common interests and concerns are intimately linked to masculine soul development. Achievement and work, athletics and exercise, and sexuality and pleasure shape a healthy spiritual attitude. In our relationships with our wives and children, the spiritual dimension is even more critical.

This is a book about spirituality, a special pathway of experience that leads us to rediscover our souls. A real-life event is spiritual if it directs us toward God, but it is mundane if the experience does not. A spiritual man is dedicated to the road that brings him closer to God, and he is ever-ready for signs of God along the way. It is not that God only emerges here and there, for God is always present. Rather, a man's developing spirituality allows him to recognize God's presence more clearly. Spirituality enhances our vision of the world. To sustain a loving relationship and be a caring, successful parent requires a soul in reasonable harmony. The inner accord comes when a man has clearly defined himself and done so in the spirit of faith in God.

Finding out who we are and who God is are our foremost challenges. I am sharing my discoveries in order to join with you in your personal quest. Together we can be assured that the soul is accessible to men as well as women. We can rediscover ourselves through our belief in the soul of man and in a God who is beyond gender concerns.

No man's personal journey is without its trials and tribulations. God foreshadowed these hardships when He spoke to our biblical forefather, Abraham: "I want you to leave your friends and relations and go to a new land" (Gen. 12:1). Abraham foretold our perspective as men when he wondered what God was leading him to. Like Abraham we also wonder.

And just as he did with Abraham, God will show us the way. He is also *our* source of direction. He walks with us on a path toward truth and discovery. He gently guides us toward the soul of man.

*David Heller*
*Boston*

# PART 1

# INFLUENCES ON THE SOUL

# CHAPTER 1

# MOTHERS AND SONS

**A**lways believe in God," my mother said to me when I was a child. "Even if God is so big that you can't see Him or even so miniature that you don't know He's there, imagine that He is. Because He really *is* there for you. And sometimes you are going to need Him very badly. Every person does. So store Him away. And never let go of Him!"

Mothers are spiritual messengers in the feminine form. They represent the origin of things and they also symbolize nature. Mothers remind us about early love and nurturance. Above all, mothers teach us at the outset about femininity and about relations with women. Few other figures in our lives are as important, and no role is more honorable than being "a joyful mother of children" (Ps. 113:9, KJV).

When we were boys, our mothers would tell us to "be careful and be home by dark." They were communicating a certain view of the world in that caring comment. When they told us that we "looked handsome," they were expressing a definite view of boys and men. And when they explained that they "were proud of us for being thoughtful," they were conveying a clear attitude about who we were as individuals and how we should behave.

But how we digest what our mothers told us varies a great deal. Some of us try to conform to our mothers' advice; others may try to do the opposite when it comes to moral and ethical behavior. Yet nearly all of us reveal the enduring signs of our mothers' influence.

Few men have had perfect relationships with their mothers and childhoods free of tension and disagreement. But how we cope with our differences, as well as what we learn from our mothers, is really a key to the reasonable growth of the soul. Because they are so prominent at the outset for most of us, mothers set the table for the kind of men we will become. Along with our fathers, our mothers' have the task of bringing us up in the "nurture of the Lord" (Eph. 6:4).

### How We Really Feel About Our Mothers

If there is one thing nearly every man is squeamish about, it's talking about his mother. Ask a man about his mother and you're bound to get a protective glare, a nervous, terse reaction, or some safe and hackneyed description. When it comes to mothers, men certainly are not verbose.

"My mother? What's there to say? She's a fine lady," exclaimed thirty-five-year-old Jim, an engineer by profession. That's how many men answer questions about their mothers. We refuse to divulge anything about our personal relationships with our mothers, as if they were conspicuously labeled top secret. But anyone who is privy to the relationship between a man and his mother knows that all kinds of intimacies, some unspoken or even unconscious, have shaped the very foundations of that man's personality.

What are some of these private memories? Their variety is as considerable as the vast array of childhood experiences can provide. But some events stay with us just below our daily awareness, such as early memories about play and pleasure, about warmth and security, confirmation or rejection, and conversations about God and the world. If mothers do not nurture a man's soul outright, they certainly can claim a pervasive and unparalled influence. Deep down most of us realize this, but we guard these early memories and sometimes keep them from even our own scrutiny.

But what motivates us to be so secretive about our mothers? Fear certainly stands at the core of our closedness, but we may hide our feelings for many different reasons. We may be afraid of understanding or reexperiencing the sense of childlike vulnerability we felt with our mothers. We may have glossed over negative feelings about our mothers, because society would consider such emotions taboo. We might feel it is unmanly to "gush" about one's mother. Or we might be made anxious as a result of the love we feel toward our mothers. Such deep feelings are sometimes hard for us to talk about.

Love and fear are powerful emotions that call forth strong feelings about our mothers. Understanding what is going on inside us will take time, but we must trust God and appreciate the meaning of "fear not, little flock" (Luke 12: 32, KJV). What is required is considerable resolve and the ability to tolerate self-examination.

"I'd like to know more about what I was like as a kid and what my mother thought of me," admitted thirty-year-old Carl, a painter. "I know it's supposed to have a big effect on you. But I wonder about little things, too. Like why I always fought with my brother, and whether my mother was really strict with us. It's a hard thing to get to the truth about. . . . Everybody has his own view of what our family was like."

## Mothers and Their Spiritual Gifts

Like Rebecca at the well, who brought physical refreshment to Abraham's servant, most of our mothers bring to us their spiritual nourishment and their gift for loving guidance. Their femininity—simple, elegant, gentle—naturally expresses itself in spirituality. They teach us in so many different ways about the earth and its creation and about a God in whom all things dwell (Col. 1:19).

Many cultures view women, and mothers in particular, as closer to nature than men. Whether such beliefs reflect cultural tradition or pinpoint the natural order of things, they encourage us to search for our spirituality and rootedness in women. Who better to turn to for these qualities than the first women in our lives, our mothers?

"My mother has a green thumb," declared twenty-year-old Keith, a college student. "But that's just because she understands how nature works. She has a real respect for the environment and for what God has given us. She taught us to remember the earth as a sign of God's genius. She says you can learn a lot about living by thinking about how creative God's world is."

Like Keith, each of us does have a story to tell about the view of the world our mothers passed on to us. Once we overcome our diffidence about talking about out mothers, a colorful collection of stories about mothers and their spiritual gifts unfolds.

One of our mothers' primary roles, for both sons and daughters, is to convey information about survival and happiness in the world. All mothers have unique points of view to impart, and as sons, we receive firsthand their unedited philosophical offerings, their special way of understanding and appreciating the world in accordance with faith and experience.

What are the most common spiritual gifts that these wise women provide for their children? Mothers communicate through their attitudes about religious service attendance and formal religion as well as their everyday manner and care for their youngsters. Mothers impart the concept of trust to their children, without which faith in life and in God is virtually impossible. Mothers instill in us a positive, a negative, or a mixed view of the world, and this shapes in unpredictable ways our appetite for social and spiritual exchange with other people. Mothers may determine whether spirituality is an acceptable idea or an irrelevant notion. They can profoundly influence whether God is a distant, mythological figure for us or an intimate, personal one who displays to us "the riches of his goodness" (Rom. 2:4).

The most important way that mothers teach us about God is through their loving care. They may not have mentioned God explicitly as they cradled us in their arms, but the heartfelt way in which they caressed us mirrored God's embrace. What a lesson we learned about love through their maternal care! It is this care that enables us to develop in a healthy way as boys and as individuals.

My mother used to sing to my brother and me so that we

would comfortably and pleasurably fall asleep. I still think of her melodies with a kind of pleasant reverie. They calm me and make me think of halcyon memories and images. They have a personal spiritualism all their own. She liked "Swing Low, Sweet Chariot" and "The Battle Hymn of the Republic" ("Mine Eyes Have Seen the Glory"). Although these selections had much lyrical substance, the way my mother sang them was a spiritual experience for me. Other mothers who may not be bedtime singers can express their loving care in other ways to their children.

Mothers also overtly convey spirituality. Each mother tailors her explanation of God with religious imagery to suit the particular needs of her son. In the best of circumstances, a flexible and continual dialogue about spirituality develops between mother and son.

"I could talk to my mother about anything," commented Michael without a hint of arrogance. Michael is a forty-year-old physician whom I knew from my graduate school days. "We used to talk about my worries, about sports, and about my friends, too. I used to ask a lot of questions, being the inquisitive kid I was. She never pushed God on me either. It was just something I was naturally curious about. And my mother always had a word or maxim that helped me. I still talk to her about my life today—only now I spend a lot of time reminding her about the things she taught me."

Although mothers differ in the spiritual education they offer, many will teach their young sons about the following: the existence of a Great Being called God; His laws and ethics and how to put them into practice; faith and self-confidence in preparation for life's journey; and the assurance of maternal support regardless of success or failure.

These are the great spiritual contributions of mothers.

They are the gifts which far outweigh the psychological obstacles that some mothers may present to their sons. How they are communicated can never be captured in a single description, for there is often a special communication between mothers and their sons. Except in unusual circumstances, that maternal practice of sharing spirituality with children has lifelong implications. We should all be thankful for the spiritual comfort of a mother.

*The Ambivalence of Men*

All boys and men share a built-in ambivalence toward their mothers that must be successfully addressed. Since mothers are also involved in training and disciplining a child, as well as nurturing him, the ambivalence is inevitable.

Since sons in infancy may be as close as daughters to their mothers, the emotional attachment of males and females is similar; however, that soon changes. In order to establish their own autonomy and eventually their own gender identity, sons tend to separate emotionally from mothers much earlier than daughters do. That detachment, to whatever degree it occurs, is always a source of considerable ambivalence on the son's part. Although a boy typically manifests an eagerness for independence and exploration, he ordinarily maintains during the early childhood years a dormant wish for continued intimacy with his mother.

That ambivalence often does not go away. In the teenage years, it may appear as a tension between schoolwork and dating. Later, as an adult, a man may experience conflict between work and family. Whatever the stage of a man's life, ambivalent feelings will emerge and cause tension within him, all because of deep conflicting feelings toward his mother. To be close or not to be close to women—that is the ambivalent question for men, as first brought about by the mother-son relationship.

This ambivalent feeling can be intense, depending on what a man's relationships with his mother and other women are like. If the women in our lives are considerate and sensitive to our needs, then the fires of conflict may diminish or die out. But if our mothers, girlfriends, and wives are difficult or insensitive at times, then the ambivalence becomes heated and aggravated. Such emotional wavering is a beneath-the-surface reason for marital discord and divorce.

Mothers can exacerbate our mixed feelings in several different ways, each of which has something to do with our self-expression. Whether it's by overt interruption or the furtive glare, mothers get their messages across. Sometimes those messages are inhibiting; often they cause frustration and tension. When men do feel comfortable enough to speak about their mothers, they convey their ambivalence.

"Don't get me wrong. I love my mother. But she's mellowed a lot," said thirty-nine-year-old Harry, a lawyer. "When I was a kid, she had a bad temper. She could be ornery at times. Once, I remember getting in trouble by playing on a neighbor's lawn. My mother kept asking me if I had anything to say for myself. Every time I tried to offer an excuse, she told me to 'shut up.'"

One way mothers can interfere with a boy's development is by verbal interruption. Verbal expression is often a part of soul expression. Even if ready-made excuses are at the tip of his tongue, a boy needs to get them out in order to get to the truth. When mothers like Harry's repeatedly present a mixed message to their children, they can cause them to be verbally constrained. The normal masculine verbal style cannot comfortably emerge. If ideas are blocked, it is highly unlikely that deeper or more enduring ideas will surface. Can such inhibition influence a man's adult behavior in work or family life? Yes. Most often, an inhibited style persists and a man finds work or social situations that accommodate his style. But he sacrifices personal development, and finding life's path is that much harder for him.

"My mother had this thing about football. Maybe it was because my father was gung ho and she did it on purpose. But she would forbid my brothers and me to play in high school," comments thirty-three-year-old Bruce, an insurance salesman. "Come to think of it, she was down on sports a lot. She used to say, if we spent as much time on homework as watching ball games, we'd all get straight A's. I'm glad I didn't listen to her."

A second common way some mothers inhibit their sons is by discouraging physical activity. For a variety of reasons, only one of which is the discomfort apparently shown by Bruce's mother, some women find it hard to relate to the ongoing physical needs of boys. Since boys appear to be more active and aggressive than girls, or at least are socialized that way, mothers often must deal with energetic and highly physical male youngsters. Some mothers, particularly those who are very passive themselves, find the level of activity uncomfortable. They try to dissuade their sons from such high-energy, nonstop play. But that parental stance can block a child's natural physical needs and his curiosity about his body and the physical world. It can create excess frustration and anxiety, which a boy may carry into adulthood. And, as occupations have grown increasingly less physical, fewer and fewer adult outlets for these physical needs exist.

The male adult who has not been able to express himself physically in a normal way may display destructive anger at a wife or child or even sink into periodic depression. Moreover, without the means of physical expression and a healthy acceptance of who he is physically, a man cannot achieve a whole sense of well-being. We cannot feel good about ourselves inwardly if we do not also feel good about ourselves physically.

A third major difficulty can be the emotional relationship between a mother and her son. For men as a whole, this is a very sensitive matter. Trevor was a twenty-seven-year-old health club instructor who had difficulty answering my questions about his mother and her effect on his life. It wasn't for lack of effort. Despite trying as hard as he could, Trevor could not crack an inner wall of stoicism. Finally he acknowledged: "Emotions were just hard to talk about in my family. Especially for the men. My mother had a hard time with them too."

A little bit of Trevor resides in most of us. That we are blocked off from our emotions is common knowledge. We have difficulty in opening up, but few of us are aware of our mothers' role in that problem. Although many women may claim that they wish men were more emotional, these same women are troubled by the feelings of boys and men. If these women came from an older generation, as our mothers did, male emotionality comes across to them as foreign and perhaps even unmanly. I believe that mothers are as involved in the control of male passions as are our fathers. Mothers can actively teach about control and strength, while fathers serve as a role model of it. Most mothers look to their daughters and husbands for social and emotional relationships, not to their sons. Thus, it is not rare for sons to exist in their own spaces within a family, emotionally close to neither mother nor father. Sadly, men are cut off from the full breath of life, which God endowed man with at Creation (Gen. 2:7).

These three types of problems between mothers and sons—the verbal, the physical, and the emotional—relate to soul development in a dramatic way. The evolution of our souls depends upon the free expression of these sides of ourselves, as well as the harmonious blending of the verbal, physical, and emotional. Complete masculinity requires that. But since some means of expression will always be blunted in childhood, it is essential to separate childhood experiences from childish ways that persist into adulthood. We can accomplish that by recognizing the vestiges of immaturity that emerge in our everyday behavior. Petulance, sarcasm, and scorn—these are the earmarks of the frustrated and the immature. Without a separation from immaturity throughout the whole being, childhood frustration will always hound us and keep us from greater fulfillment. It is not a matter of age or marital status; it's a matter of men's spiritual growth. Sometimes a man must recognize the biblical wisdom of giving up childish ways (1 Cor. 13:11).

*Separating the Man from the Boy*

The separation of a man from boyish traits is really the same as a psychological peace about his parents in general and his mother in particular. Each is achieved in the same way: through will, dedication, and belief in the autonomy and integrity of the self. But a man can imagine that kind of separation easier than accomplish it. It requires an understanding of our mothers' various influences on us and a perceptiveness about how that affects us in a contemporary way. We must know ourselves, and know the roots we come from, too, yet be willing to give up the past for future gain (Phil. 3:5–8).

If our natural drives are impeded, wouldn't it make sense to get roundly angry and just act as we wish? Perhaps. But the nature of mother-son relations and their impact is more complicated than that.

Anger is important; it can free us from debilitating attachments. That doesn't mean getting rid of our mothers! It suggests the need to sever whatever neurotic or self-defeating ties we have to our mothers. It implies the need to express the natural upset and outrage at being held back in some way as a child. Our mothers may have discouraged us from being openly masculine and kept us from exhibiting our budding masculine gestures and postures. We must protest. We owe that to ourselves.

With regard to our mothers, anger is hardly the main theme in our relationships with them. Recall that God's anger "endures but a moment" (Ps. 30:5). Our deep love for our mothers makes our ambivalence all the more entrenched and painful. It's also why anger is not sufficient for a smooth separation. We must realize and accept the positive contributions our mothers have made. They have taught us to love and to give, and those two related acts bring us closer to God. Mothers have instilled in us the right qualities that can make us "children of light" (John 12:36). Separation, and therefore adulthood, requires an honest appreciation and thankfulness for benevolent mothering.

Feeling love and disappointment simultaneously is hard for most of us. But if we can feel both, we can courageously experience both sides of ourselves, and that's a vital step on the way to soul development. "He that overcomes shall inherit all things," including the restoration of the soul (Rev. 21:7).

To the extent that ambivalence is not resolved, we will retain the characteristics of our youth—rebellion, uncertainty, and fear. Whether we call them boyishness or immaturity, those annoying traits have to diminish if we want to sustain a meaningful place in the world and pass along a sound legacy to our children. We exemplify this boyishness by needing to impress others in the same way we first tried to impress our mothers and by reacting childishly and selfishly.

Leaving behind boyishness also means refusing to engage in silly battles of control with our girlfriends and wives, just as we once may have fought with our mothers. The boy in us will assuredly depart if we relinquish distorted or embellished ideas we carry about our mothers. Reality has a way of curing many psychological confusions. Accepting our mothers as people, complete with their own strengths and weaknesses, can go a long way in helping us live maturely and spiritually.

Manhood demands an adult relationship with our mothers, but just as important, mature relations with the other women in our lives. Since many men find their soulfulness in their intimate relationships, a healthy separation from childhood opens the spiritual door. The enlightened man is one who can love and experience life unencumbered by the anxieties of the past. To be able to say "I love you" to a female partner with sincerity, we must put to rest the leftover inhibitions of an earlier era. The fortunate among us realize that there is a world beyond ambivalence, but it resides just at the juncture where we accept our own individuality. Ultimately we detach our own psychological umbilical cords and determine what our life will be like. A person is responsible for his life and for his own beliefs.

### My Own Mother

As I have gone through inner changes in regard to my childhood and my views of women, my relationship with my own mother has changed accordingly. We've had our harmonious periods, and we've had our disagreements as well. We've had our share of laughter and poignant moments, too. There has been a great deal of ebb and flow in our mother-son relationship. But somehow we've both survived my need for psychological exploration. Most likely, we are both the better for it.

My mother likes to say that we have always gotten along well. But the reality is that it is only now, after many years of attempting to understand myself and her, that we really appreciate the impact we have had on each other. Mothers shape their sons, and sons influence their mothers. And we spend most of our lives not fully aware of how profoundly we can affect each other.

Today I'm able to talk with my mother openly. But that isn't really the most important thing. As my mother would undoubtedly say, "Just as long as you're happy, that's what matters."

Happiness is an important part of a man's life, and separation from past obstacles is key. But forging that type of spiritual separation offers other benefits. My relationship with my mother now is more soulful and richer than ever before. Very quietly, the relationships in my life have become increasingly deeper and clearer. The old fears about intimacy pop up from time to time, but my will to be creative and forward-looking supplants them. I've done my best to make peace with the mother I remembered from childhood and have opened myself to the opportunities that now emerge. My mother will always be a significant person in my life, but I am the force that determines the course of my life. I have chosen God as the center from which my life unfolds, just as the soulful man of Bible times saw the heavenly Jerusalem, the city of God, as the mother of us all (Gal. 4:26).

*The Roots of My Spirituality*

I was fortunate to be brought up by both my mother and my grandmother (my maternal grandmother). These two women gave my brother and me a great deal of love and attention. That was the primary way they taught us about God. But they also talked to us specifically about God—what God did, what God might be like, why it was important to believe in God. My early conversations with both of them, sometimes over a bowl of cereal or a peanut butter and jelly sandwich, have found their way into my conversations about religion and my writing. I owe them a great deal when it comes to my understanding of God and my life's philosophy. "Pleasant words are as an honeycomb, sweet to the soul, and health to the bones" (Prov. 16:24, KJV), and their spiritual food was an abiding source of sustenance for me.

As I have thought back over these conversations, a number of discoveries about God stand out. As my mother might say: "Some things just sound true to a person. Listen for those. And if a saying or idea doesn't ring true for you, then maybe it's for someone else."

*Thirty Things My Mother (and Grandmother)*
*Told Me About God*

1. Don't expect God to be introduced by loud noises and colorful miracles. God comes to us in all kinds of ways.

2. Always be gracious and open to guests, for they may be carrying God's spirit with them.

3. Try to grow up and be a man in *God's* eyes, not in the eyes of other people.

4. God wants us to enjoy playing as well as working.

5. Learn to be familiar with what is in your heart, for that is where God resides. "Where the Spirit of the Lord is, there is liberty" (2 Cor. 3:17, KJV).

6. Look for God in other people as well as yourself.

7. God gives everyone special talents, but it is up to you to realize them.

8. If it bothers a person that he can't see God, then he should listen for Him.

9. God walks with us (and runs when necessary) throughout our lives.

10. God has no favorites. We are all His favorites.

11. God is beyond mothers, fathers, and grandparents. It is good for a person to accept the humanness of his parents and accept them as a blessing. One generation can bless another (Gen. 28:14).

12. When God said, "Honor your mother and father," He meant be respectful to all of your elders as if they were your parents. And He wants you to respect yourself, too.

13. Through our love we begin to learn what God's love is like.

14. If you feel far away from God, walk by a river or the ocean and think about how they came to be. "The earth is the Lord's and the fullness thereof" (Ps. 24:1).

15. Many different religions and cultures around the world have something valuable to offer about God.

16. In God's view, men and women are the same, even though they may express themselves in different ways.

17. Look for goodness in other people and you are likely to find goodness in yourself.

18. What God wants for you may be different from what God wants for anybody else, so expect the unexpected.

19. Care about and help people who are troubled or in pain; it's the most important thing you can do. It is also the best way to feel good about yourself.

20. Politeness is God's idea of being stylish.

21. Don't expect the important things in life to come quickly. But never give up on having them either.

22. It is important to believe in yourself, for God doesn't create anyone He doesn't believe in. God has respect for us (Lev. 26:9).

23. If you can learn to forgive, you have the ability to grow closer to God. It is "exalted to offer forgiveness" (Acts 5:31).

24. A family is one way that God helps us discover more about Him. It is sensible to be thankful for the family.

25. It is good to be flexible about what God may be like, for you will grow more knowledgeable as you collect life experiences. We are all "as clay in the potter's hand" (Jer. 18:6).

26. Don't take popular and simple notions of God too seriously.

27. Don't push away religious ideas just because they are foreign to you; don't embrace them because they seem current and exciting.

28. It is not where you live that matters, but rather what lives in *you* that counts.

29. Doing God's work is more important than talking about God's work.

30. Remember your mother fondly. God created her, too, both for you and for the people in her life and yours.

# CHAPTER 2

# THE
# EVERLASTING
# FATHER

**W**hile I was in graduate school at the University of Michigan, I had the good fortune to meet with Hans Küng—the noted Catholic theologian who wrote *On Being a Christian, Freud and the Problem of God,* and then later, *Does God Exist?* At the time, Reverend Küng was on sabbatical and had accepted a lectureship at Michigan. I was beginning my dissertation on children's images of God. I wanted to meet this man for several reasons, not the least of which was my hunger for depth and insight. He had also taken on a symbolic significance for me. Owing to his Germanic background and his obvious zealousness about religion, I had equated Küng in my fantasy world with my father, whose Holocaust history and occasional religious fanaticism were indelibly part of my early family life. When I left my apartment on an unusually clear Ann Arbor day in January of 1984, I did not know if

I was meeting Hans Küng because he seemed similar to my father or because he seemed close to God.

As I knocked on Küng's hotel room door at the Ann Arbor Inn, I first noticed the curious red and gold Minnesota crest emblazoned across the entrance, a tribute to a Big Ten football rival. This out-of-place insignia stirred images of masculine confrontations of a less sublime order. Apparently, in this Midwest bastion of sports where football was a religion, Küng had been assigned the Minnesota room. "How funny," I thought. I laughed nervously and innocently at the logo, with no premonition that Minnesota would emerge again and again in my life and ultimately be the first site of my public lecturing about children and religion.

Reverend Küng greeted me with a slight European accent and a warm smile. At once I shook in ambivalence. His speech reminded me of my father's, but his overriding personal manner suggested something else. Küng had a far greater peace about him. We sat down promptly, and he spoke freely. We engaged in a variety of typical academic discussions, concerning such provocative matters as gender differences in God imagery and papal infallibility. Throughout, I listened with interest, but my attentiveness turned to unqualified awe when Küng spoke about fathers and their godlike influence on religious beliefs.

"It is important not to underestimate the influence of our fathers on belief or doubt," he asserted. "For all his genius, Freud believed that there was no God. This was because of his own neuroses. Freud's relation to his father was extremely ambivalent, and it did not allow him to see the eternal Father. In trying to rid himself of his own father, or his father's effect on him, he tried to erase the existence of God. Of course, that's impossible." Küng took a moment to allow the silence to echo his views and then looked up at me. "Is that similar to your views, David?"

I didn't know what to say in response. In that moment I felt very bewildered. Amazingly, Küng's theoretical analyses of Freud seemed to touch on the very issues I had been struggling with on a personal level. But how did Küng know? Was it a mere coincidence? Was I granting him too much paternal respect and power, or was he, in truth, divinely inspired?

I am still not certain. I do recall that Küng went on to talk about the repression of religion and about men's struggles with one another, or, as his young nephew put it: "Uncle Hans's fights with the pope." I remember that as I was leaving, he asked me where my father was born. With a knowing look, Küng met my eyes with care and patted me gently on the back as he said, "You have a difficult task ahead of you, but you are a man who is well prepared for what awaits you." When we shook hands and parted, I felt deeply changed. I am tempted to say that a torch had been passed to me, but really it was more like a lightning bolt. I suddenly knew that anything is possible if you have faith (Mark 9:23).

This meeting with Hans Küng was an important lesson for me in accepting my own wish to be closer to my father and in understanding my ongoing search for God. I was confused about what I was looking for in life, and this memorable episode helped to clarify things. Fortunately, Küng provided both the missing parental support and the spiritual gift of vision. Since that meeting, I have learned that my confusion is something that many men unconsciously share. I now believe that it is a fundamental task for men to distinguish between the images of their fathers and their images of God. For a man to become a fully spiritual person, he must learn this critical difference and fully explore his own religious beliefs. It may sound simple, but the path to selfhood and fulfillment is quite rocky. And yet, "happy are those who strive for peace, they shall be called the sons of God" (Matt. 5:9).

Until I met Hans Küng and began studying God images, I wasn't aware of my own beliefs about God. I realized only then that my image of God was benevolent but was also scarred by negative expectations and fears. I thought that God must be a helping force, but I wondered if God was sometimes punishing and dictatorial. Was God really on my side? If God was, what was the other side that I imagined? For the first time I was seriously examining my inner life.

It wasn't long before I began to understand some of the roots of my God image. I began to explore the other side of the soul. My father, or rather my childhood image of my father, indeed had heavily shaped my religious ideas.

My father was often harsh and punitive. He demanded that I heed his words, particularly concerning religious rituals and practices, or suffer the consequences of his displeasure. As a child, I was perplexed by him as much as I feared him. Sometimes he would avoid me. Sometimes he would lash out with physical anger. And, when he was feeling especially bad about himself, as he did on occasion, he would simply tell me that I was no good. I could feel the pain of his words for years to come. I knew that it would be a long time before my scars healed.

He told me about his Holocaust experiences, too, and I fantasized even more. Awful images of death and anguish were painfully accessible. I wanted to push them away but couldn't. The need to make sense of them was compelling and powerful. Implicit in my personal psychology was a tremendous confusion, inherited from my father, about why the unspeakable destruction had occurred. "Why" was the un-forgettable echoing word of my childhood. Pain and rage and not knowing were inseparable for my father; they were always part of me. I learned to silently wonder about the dreaded question: "What kind of God caused that hell?"

My father carried with him some sense of an overbearing and cruel God, and I picked it up from him. Maybe, given his extreme experiences as the sole survivor in his family, his insensitive and erratic behavior was comprehensible. But his experiences dominated my early life. They influenced how I saw the world, and they distorted my image of God as well. All of this influence was difficult enough, but there was an additional confusion in my soul. I could never explain why my father, with his outrage and guilt and despair, had sur-vived and persisted in his belief in a God.

The Küng meeting changed the way I thought about religion. Küng pointed me in a direction of a thoroughly benign God, a vision I had been searching for without realiz-ing. The theologian's kindness touched me; his wisdom in-structed me. I now had a better idea of how my father had indirectly colored my view of God. The conversation with Küng helped cleanse me spiritually and inspired me to take a fresh look at God. Ultimately it opened me up to myself and to the soulful experiences of other men. It led me to realize that "the door is [indeed] open to everyone who knocks" (Luke 11:9).

*Father or Heavenly Father?*

The confusion over fathers and the paternal image of God is something that I have often observed since that mem-orable meeting with Hans Küng. Perhaps that meeting made me more aware of my own uncertainties, but I have also witnessed similar tension in many other men. During my internships in clinical psychology, I saw a number of male patients whose ambivalent feelings toward their fathers confounded their religious ideas and their views of the world. I talked at length with several male colleagues and friends, men who came from widely disparate religious backgrounds, each of whom was trying to sort out his own sense of masculinity and his own spiritual beliefs. Taking the subject to heart and studying it in a more formal way, I began to interview men concerning their expectations about God. Although my first questions were often met with incredulous, blank stares, the God imagery of men is ultimately quite revealing about their relationships to their fathers and their ongoing search for peace.

But how do relationships with our fathers fit into the greater spiritual scheme of things? Why do they enhance or inhibit our spiritual development even through the adult years?

If a man's soul is linked to his discovery of God, then significant experiences that lead him to this discovery are paramount. Fathers represent to most of us a living tie to ancestry and history, because fathers carry with them the family surname and the seeds of continuity as well. Fathers should provide direction about how to look for God, not only through ritual and custom, but by teaching us how to be men. But that isn't always easy. Our fathers had their own dilemmas to work out, and the popular definitions of manhood may not be the same as manhood in the eyes of God. But fathers can play a decisive role in sifting through the wheat and chaff of ideas about manhood. They can provide us with a spiritual compass with which to live. "A good man has a firm footing" (Prov. 10:9).

There is also another element in the father-son relationship that is essential to spirituality—male intimacy. Many men seem to have a considerable problem with it. Most of us are afraid of intimacy. We learned that fear from our fathers, and now it can insidiously find its way into our relationships with other men and with women. But more important, if we cannot be close to our brothers and sisters, how can we expect to be close to God?

"The way to a godly life is no easy matter" (1 Tim. 3:16). Our journey toward God begins with the earliest experiences of warmth and love from our fathers, along with our mothers. Through their guidance we first learn to relate to other people and to God. Their capacity for caring and closeness reveals the first clues of what the world may be like. They teach us through their actions and manner about human kinship and the common heritage we share under God. Too often, however, problems in the father-son exchange create anxieties about intimacy and cloud our sense of direction.

For male children the seeds of a dilemma sprout early. Unlike their female counterparts, boys at ages four and five usually experience strong feelings of rivalry and camaraderie with their fathers. The wish for closeness and identification with their fathers motivates boys throughout the growing years. Yet the wish to compete and to better his father in both physical and intellectual tests compels a youngster, too. Reconciling conflicting interests is not always a smooth process, though a healthy vision of the world and a realistic appreciation of its Creator depend on its successful resolution. Without a satisfactory merging of our positive and negative feelings toward our fathers, we cannot sustain spiritual faith. If we are willing to correct our distorted viewpoints, we can be "on the pathway to life" (Prov. 10:17).

A boy's fantasies about his father are boundless. In looking back into our childhoods, we should all ask: "How did
I imagine my father?" "How did I picture God?"

Tom, age twelve, illustrated in his spontaneous comments how father feelings can find their way into a boy's
religious imagery. Tom undeniably placed his father on a
pedestal. Tom's father, though working ten-hour days, remained a dominant figure in the household. Tom revered
him to an extreme, perhaps with the hope that such reverence would bring them closer together. When I asked Tom
about his ideas concerning God, the impact of his father was
transparent. "God is a big, tall guy with real long legs," Tom
explained with great confidence. "He works hard taking care
of the world all day, stopping a flood or moving a mountain
and stuff like that. He's got a lot of power, but people on
earth see it only once a year, at Christmas." Like that of so
many boys, Tom's imagery shows how he tried to make sense
of his father's activities. Like other twelve-year-olds, Tom
will carry these ideas with him into adolescence.

During the adolescent years when most boys exhibit independence and even rebellion, they sometimes deny a father's importance. If you ask teenage boys about it, they
often aren't so sure about their concept of God, either. They
see authority figures, earthly or divine, as the enemy. Boys
imagine that these older male forces constrain them. They
seek free expression of their social and sexual desires, and
unconsciously, their spiritual yearnings, too. Turning to their
peers to be sanctioned as males, boys make "the group"
more important than family or a relationship to God.

Daniel, age fifteen, described an image of God that cap-
tures two prevailing themes of adolescence for boys; loneli-

ness and the search for male identity. Concerning the Creation story, Daniel offered this personalized account: "Maybe God was lonely, so He made something like earth, where man would be. And He got lonelier, so He began making man and animals. He took dirt and He made it in the form of man. Something happened and man came to life."

Daniel's interpretation of how manhood comes about, clearly woven into his biblical rendition, also reveals a cry for help. He would very much like a father figure to magically guide him through this period of growing up. Like many adolescents, however, Daniel also pushes away his father and older males in his life. Actually, he wants to become like them and feels he must do so without the assistance of adults, a lonely path to pursue. Even though we, like Daniel, may try to hide our feelings, "God knows the secrets of every heart" (Ps. 44:21).

During their early twenties, most men recognize their father's significance, and some grapple with the notion of God. Yet entering the adult world and creating a niche for themselves occupies most of their attention. Most young men don't fully perceive that their initial career and family choices have something to do with their fathers, or with their God images for that matter. Our decisions may depend on these images, however, for a young man unknowingly wants his father's sanction. He hopes that his life plan, even if tentative, will exist in harmony with God's intentions for him.

A young man focuses on proving himself in the world and acquiring the accoutrements of masculinity—power and money. Possessing these worldly treasures may allow him to feel more masculine and equal to his father, but they rarely guarantee lasting satisfaction. Proving their masculinity unfortunately obsesses some men in their twenties and leads to a futile quest to prove something to a father. Such pursuits often drive a young man further from God. He may learn too late that the "soul is far too precious to be ransomed by mere earthly wealth" (Ps. 49:9).

A good friend went through such a conflict in proving himself. At twenty-four, Don had married a woman from his hometown and had recently become the father of a newborn son. He was working toward a doctorate in the humanities and seemed quite content with his new domestic life. On more than one occasion, Don emphasized that he believed that God was at the center of his life. Yet rather abruptly Don, who was peaceful by nature, decided to enlist in the National Guard. His choice would take him away from his family on weekends throughout the year and then for the greater part of the summer.

Don's rationale was that he needed to make some extra money now that the baby had arrived. But guilt over becoming a father and the desire for his own father's confirmation may well have truly shaped his decision. Don's father was a war veteran who advocated "toughness" at all costs. With the voice of his father still loud and declarative inside, Don pulled away from his tranquil existence and from the life he was building.

With the prospect of live bullets in training bringing him closer to reality, Don's conflict surfaced. Gradually he realized his choice was self-defeating and that he could solidify his masculinity in more personally satisfying ways. Realizing he did not have the ultimate power "to map his life" (Jer. 10:23), he recentered himself spiritually and became a deacon at his church. Even his father, the embodiment of masculinity for Don, approved of the direction Don pursued.

Once a man achieves a certain stability in the world—perhaps in his late twenties or early thirties—discriminating between God and earthly figures needs to be at the forefront. Lamentably, many of us do not make this distinction a priority. Confusions manifest themselves in work, in family life, and in our religious beliefs as well.

We have many images of God. Understanding how psychological fantasy weaves itself into these images can be the first step to truly knowing God. With this knowledge can come healing, for God, who knows the masculine soul because He created it, "will heal us . . . He will set us on our feet again" (Hos. 6:1–2).

### The God Images of Adult Men

When speaking about God, men project onto the Lord many of the feelings they still harbor toward their fathers. Although a God figure is highly personalized, resting at the core of our individuality, we can recognize some clear and widespread images that distort the reality of God.

One common image is "the senior executive." Those of us who imagine God as a business executive share a few common traits, and we reflect these in our fantasy ideas about God. We picture God as highly task-oriented and pragmatic, an efficient but somewhat distant authority figure. Years ago this God planned the world and implemented His grand design. In the twentieth century, He merely watches over His subordinates, who include national and international leaders. This Deity is by no means a despot, but He does insist that His work be accomplished, and charges men to do that. Every man has his own job, as prescribed by God's design. God's main concern is an orderly and prosperous world, so that goal is the business of everyday life for mankind.

The fact that God in this view is a nine-to-five being means that men must often make decisions for themselves, something that they accept begrudgingly. Although God commands great respect from us, He is not a demonstrative or emotional Deity. Except for wars, marriage, and other important human events, He rarely intervenes. God's gray hair signifies His distinguished position, but it also indicates a certain blandness that some of us see in the world.

Thirty-seven-year-old Martin, a businessman, described a God that resembled "God, the senior executive." "I imagine that God is at the helm of the earth, which is part of a larger corporation like on the old 'Star Trek' series. I'm not sure that we can see God that much in our lives; maybe they could in the times of the Bible. But He—I guess it's fashionable to say He or She—makes sure that things work out. Obviously, everything is not perfect these days, but I believe it would be if we could follow God's plan. It's easy to lose sight of what we're put on earth to achieve."

Martin's God appears as a reasonably positive force that offers initial direction and then sets man to work things out. Like many men, Martin had respected his own father but never felt quite close enough to him. He still believes quite strongly in his father's conservative values and way of life, but he does not feel he has lived up to his father's expectations. Martin's fantasy description of God is really a portrait of his father in real life. Martin would very much like to feel more like his father does. Beneath his objective appraisal of the world, Martin actually feels quite guilty for disappointing his father. He realizes that he is not perfect, and he loses sight of what his goals are.

A second way men describe God is "God, the head of the

divine household." Unlike the executive Deity, this God consistently involves Himself in the world's affairs. The earth is in fact God's territory, and heaven is His vacation retreat, a charming villa on a spiritual mountaintop. God not only sets down the rules for people's conduct, but also ensures that His wishes are carried out. He rewards the obedient and punishes the disobedient.

This Deity has considerable power, but it's not absolute. He discusses matters with His descendants on earth. Nevertheless, His preferences, based on wisdom and governed by justice and mercy, are the deciding factors in any earthly consideration. We can imagine this God figure at the designated end of the supper table, delivering pragmatic philosophy about life. When God speaks, everyone must listen. Since His affairs are never mundane, He undoubtedly influences everyone's life.

"I picture the Lord as a man," offered twenty-nine-year-old Bill, an electrician. "Being a Christian, I imagine Him in a human form, sitting around in a big easy chair smoking a pipe. He's pretty much a peaceful God, except when He gets upset and people don't listen to Him. He always has control of any situation. That's why He's 'God'! I guess you learn these ideas early on and they stay with you. Somebody else might have a different idea about what God is like."

Bill easily conjures up this image of God. Bill grew up in a religious family where respect for the Lord as well as courtesy to elders were taken for granted. Bill's father did smoke a pipe, in fact, and frequently sat on a recliner in the living room designated by the family as "Dad's Chair." Bill's father controlled the family. Bill and his four siblings answered to their father in all major aspects of their lives as children. Bill and the others quietly resented his authority, but at the same time felt grateful for their father's interest and involvement.

Although there may be some truth in Bill's view, God is not just the head of a household. "He lives in us" (Heb. 3:6), and is not just a figure of authority.

Some others portray God as the Mighty Hulk, a physically dominant but ordinarily benign figure. In this interpretation, God can move whole continents and alter the physical laws of the world if He so desires. For such men, God is the same spiritual being who made the sun stand still and parted the Red Sea. But perhaps the most fitting biblical scenario is the image of a Deity who, empowered with great strength, aided Samson when he moved the colossal pillars of the pagan temple. The forces that oppose Him, which can include a whole host of earthly bullies, stand no real chance against His mighty will.

In this portrayal, God protects against evil. He watches over smaller and weaker beings, like women and children, who are deemed worthy and needy of His care. He is ageless but very human at the same time. He is muscular and sturdy, "a man's God" who is ever prepared for superheroic feats. He is the combination of a wrestler and a theologian, with His ultimate purpose linked to spiritual trial and combat.

"God is one big dude," quipped twenty-seven-year-old Joe, a salesman. "But I don't mean to be a wise guy. I think of Hercules; God makes sure people keep in line. With all that's going on in the world today, with so much violence and all, God's got to be a pretty tough cookie! I think maybe He adjusts to the way the world is at any given date. By the year two thousand, who knows what God will be like? Maybe He'll blow His cool," Joe concluded with a wry grin.

So like many men who grow up in blue-collar families, Joe was surrounded by men who emphasized the physical. The family equated physical prowess and strength with masculinity. His father was a mason, and though Joe went on to work in an office, highly physical outdoor activities such as hunting and fishing dominated his hobbies. A tall, broad-shouldered man, Joe's father is still considered "the rock of the family." His father could usually be counted on in a crisis or difficult circumstances, and this shaped Joe's image of God.

Men who grow up with weak or absent fathers may also imagine such a Herculean God. In this way, God becomes a wished-for figure that makes up for the missing father figure. This God exhibits standard paternal functions like strength or protection, but often does so in an exaggerated manner. He may be invoked to help us through the hard times.

A fourth way men depict God is as "God, the divine referee." Unlike the preceding Deity figures, this fourth image stands decidedly neutral. God scrutinizes the actions of men and women with great tenacity and records their behaviors with inspired vision and divine recall. God "calls them as He sees them," never interfering while human events unfold. Because people have complete freedom, God holds them entirely accountable for their choices. If a person should deceive or injure someone else, then God will deliver justice and penalize the guilty party.

God's impartiality makes Him a respected but controversial figure. His looming presence and His oversight role insure that He possesses great authority. Although He is reputed to be eminently fair in His judgments, some of us differ with Him on occasion. We feel He doesn't understand us or hear our explanations. Yet others accept God's authority without question, and recognize the need for benign arbitration.

Supposedly God officiates at selected religious sites, where people congregate to praise God's just and fair work. He posts religious guidelines or commandments in His divine rule book. At the end of our lives, God checks His spiritual scorecard, sums up our personal pluses and minuses, and determines our fate. If we abide by His rules, God then grants us an "overtime period" after our time on earth has expired.

Thomas, age forty-three and a lawyer, revealed such a God concept. In his view, the Deity was not the God of formal religion but the real-world God of his own experiences. Despite expressing some skepticism, Thomas portrayed a neutral God.

"God? Well, I don't believe in the God of churches and ministers," Thomas began. "I do think that there is a superior being, though. It's a guiding body. I think that it's there to make sure people get along and do things according to the way that's orderly. People like to argue, and God is there to make certain it doesn't get out of control. We need an objective force looking after us. Maybe God helps you stay within your limits."

His parents' discord and eventual divorce disrupted Thomas's own early life. Although he was never out of contact with his father after the divorce, their relationship remained distant and their meetings infrequent unless a major event brought them together. Once, when Thomas injured himself in a high school football game, he saw his father every day for a week. Otherwise the contact was intermittent and neutral, a dry report of school and athletic activities rather than a warm father-and-son exchange.

As an adult, Thomas's own marriage has held together despite numerous flare-ups. Thomas and his wife have different personalities, and they disagree often. Managing his impulsivity has been a lifelong concern for Thomas, particularly in intimate relationships, and his image of God seems to play a prominent role in his self-control. Although Thomas is visibly negative, he still expresses a belief and hope that life is worth living.

But Thomas's view of God is inaccurate, because God is not neutral. God cares about us. "He hears the cry of those being oppressed" (Job 34:28).

In addition to these relatively positive or ambivalent images of God, some men picture God as "the angry father." This fantasy creation, a nightmarish tyrant, haunts a person and dictates his actions. Dominance and villainy typify this God.

Authoritarian and self-centered, guided by ego and insatiable greed, God, the angry father, acts arbitrarily and without advance warning. Lightning, thunderbolts, and plagues are part of His arsenal. He shows little concern for humanity or for the perpetuation of any values, aside from His own hedonistic gain. This Deity is power-hungry. Despite His awesome dominion, He never seems content. He makes incessant and unreasonable demands on humanity.

The angry, virulent God mistreats His children and punishes them frequently. Harsh in demeanor, He uses intimidation freely and indiscrimately. As His children, we are required to obey, but He sends wars, disasters, and famines in return. We are expected to love the Deity precisely because He has power over us; we must never question His authority. Even if we hate Him clandestinely and lament our predicament, we must conceal our true feelings for our own safety.

"What kind of God would have us go into Vietnam or have the marines killed in Lebanon?" questioned fifty-year-old Jack, a supermarket manager. "You have to wonder about God sometimes. I often feel like saying, 'God, thanks a lot for all the mess you've made.' He must like a lot of action. Why else would He create so much pain and trouble? Why did He let people die in the Holocaust? Let's face it: the world is no democracy. If God isn't dead, he's a monster!"

Jack's personal history unveils a pattern consistent with his troublesome notion of God. Jack's father, an extremely harsh and tyrannical man, controlled Jack's meek mother and each of the five children. His father hit Jack throughout his childhood, often without reason. On several painful occasions, Jack spoke back to his inebriated father, and was then forced to flee to a neighbor's home for safety. Jack stopped speaking to his father after he turned twenty, and only related the details of his early years with great reluctance.

In adulthood, Jack remains bitter about his background. But he also identifies with his father more than he likes to admit. He demands unflinching respect from his three children and angrily resents their independent strivings. He complains about their habits and manners repeatedly. Jack seems firmly entrenched in a negative view of the world, and is ever vigilant about all those he encounters.

In contrast to these mistaken ideas, God is not an angry, bitter figure. God is not the incarnation of wrath. "God is not unfair" (Heb. 6:10). God is anything but such negative images. "The Lord is merciful and gracious, slow to anger, and plenteous in mercy. He will not always chide: neither will he keep his anger for ever" (Ps. 103:8–9, KJV).

The various God images may appear in combination in a given individual. They indicate that images rooted in childhood are long-lasting, with regard both to our fathers and to God. A large part of what we imagine is based on what we learn from others, but not everything. Imagination also requires faith. Ironically, faith can also be our greatest ally if our faith is attached to the reality of God.

In order to shed misleading Deity fantasy images, we must make peace with our earthly fathers. Although finding a new and true image of God may be a difficult task for many of us, the best way to accomplish this is to think through our relations with our fathers. We must ask ourselves in as earnest a way as possible: "How has my relationship with my father affected who I am?" "How has that relationship affected who I would like to become?" Only through answering these tough questions can we get to know God all the better. And remember that "knowing God results in every other kind of understanding" (Prov. 9:10).

*A Man's Journey*

"A time to find, a time to lose," those ageless words from Ecclesiastes (3:6), poetically portray our journey of discovery. Letting go of childhood relationships with our fathers brings pain. We must depart from these old ways of seeing and make room for a new outlook on life and beyond.

This new vision has many names and descriptions, but whatever it is called, it centers itself around a deep and serious faith in God. And the faith is always a personal faith, a set of beliefs accepted as one's own.

If a person is fortunate, he may be able to find other good

people to guide him in his journey. In all walks of life, there are good people around us. We just have to keep an eye out for them. Hans Küng was one of those people for me. He would occasionally send me a paper or some personal greetings, in response to receiving my books. The essence of the exchange, though intangible at times, was meaningful to me. With this sharing of ideas, I received some of the spiritual nourishment that I yearned for. Reverend Küng was helping me to look for God in my own life.

Küng had much to offer concerning God, but I was responsible for discerning from his harvest of ideas the truth for my own heart. I have learned that we can find God in our personal histories and in our everyday experiences. Even when we question what it means to be a man, God is there. God is our ally as we resist the temptation of superficial and ephemeral masculine trends. God helps us concentrate on our spiritual essence, given to us by Him. He is our great source of strength; He inspires us to accomplish great things.

Although God may be on our side, we're not always sure we want to side with God, who often becomes confused with our fathers or other human figures. Too often we keep our distance from God. We vacillate between faith and doubt, skeptically asking ourselves whether our longings and prayers might not be fruitless. Personally, I feared that I would reach manhood but lose "my soul in the process" (Mark 9:36). I have since discovered that it was an unfounded fear.

In my efforts as a writer, I have known spiritual quagmires and internal prisons, but by implication, Reverend Küng and others have encouraged me to continue writing. I write as much for those without faith or understanding as for those who have both. In the different stages of my own journey, I have sometimes lacked faith or understanding, but

I have survived, and my soul is the better for my experiences. "The Lord will not let a good man starve to death," physically or spiritually (Prov. 10:3).

"Where in my immediate life can I experience God more vividly?" I have often wondered.

I learned through the experience with Reverend Küng that I can look for God in my relations with other men, including my father. Certainly that must be true for all men. God exists in the way that we care about each other. God exists in a warm slap on the back or a firm handshake. God is there as we embrace each other after a long absence.

But I also discovered from Hans Küng that God emerges in more subtle ways. God is with us when things are tough or when we are thwarted, as is the case with an illness, a professional problem, or the failure of a relationship. Like a good father, God makes sure we are not alone. In these dire situations, God can help. God can create new perspectives and a new outlook for us even when the circumstances seem hopeless.

Yet God emerges in our lives when things are going smoothly, too. God can make sure things run of their own accord. This is the experience of God's nurturance and companionship. God is like the father who takes care of things for his son. God befriends us and ensures our happiness.

God also exists in our experiences of kinship and familiarity with other men, even men from distant lands. When we feel a relation to people or events that can't readily be explained, then we are moved to wonder: could God be involved? Indeed God is intimately involved with the spiritual connectedness of all men, such as with the link I felt with Hans Küng across the globe.

If I could summarize what I have discovered, I would

express it this way: Our paternalistic notions of God can never do God justice. God is beyond our imaginations and yet paradoxically accessible to us at the same time. But we must not be neutral about God. We must trust and believe in the God of goodness and infinite possibilities, not a limited God prone to shortcomings. We must also understand that love is the seal of each of our covenants with God. "All the special gifts and powers from God will someday come to an end, but love goes on forever" (1 Cor. 13:8).

Even if we accept love as the seal of our relationship to God, how does it help us make peace with our fathers?

A solid belief in God's love allows us to love our fathers and treat them with compassion. We can more easily forgive them for their sins, and forgive ourselves, too. Dedicated to love, we can feel the gratitude for the positive things our fathers have given to us. We can appreciate their humanness more fully, for we understand that their spiritual needs are similar to ours. As men, we stand with our fathers before God and realize that both of us are the "sons of God" (Rom. 8:14).

In so many ways a father's spiritual contribution is like a mother's contribution. The gifts of nurturance and guidance are evident in their spiritual parenting. But because we share a common gender with our fathers, our sense of identification is that much more profound. We pick up so much from our fathers about how to act and how to live. Our very beings are shaped by their manner and behavior. Yet even such important identifications must ultimately give way to a greater identification with God.

God is "the everlasting Father" (Isa. 9:6) who guides us toward a whole and spiritual sense of manhood. God is there to inspire us, console us, and confirm us. He accompanies us on our life journey, from the first steps we risk as toddlers until our final hours as men. We give glory to God by walking in His footsteps, by following in His image.

God moves us to say: "I will not be alone, for the Father is with me" at all times (John 16:32). God is there for you and me and for all men, offering His blessing to His beloved sons.

# CHAPTER 3

# BOY'S COURAGE, MAN'S COURAGE

**Y**ou can measure a man by how willing he is to go out on a limb," said Bert, a forty-one-year-old construction foreman. "I really admire a guy like Lee Iacocca. Because he said he was dedicated to saving Chrysler and he went out and did it. That took a lot of determination and fearless action."

Men enjoy talking about courage more than about most other topics. We may not call it courage; more likely, we call it "guts." But we know what a fellow like Bert is talking about when he describes some feat he admires. He's speaking about some act of unusual risk taking, well-conceived or otherwise, that makes us halt and take notice. Whether it's mountain climbing or public speaking, we love to think about the men who stand out from the crowd.

What fascinates us so much about courage? Several factors seem to be at work. As Bert implied, we use courage as a criterion with which to evaluate other men as well as ourselves. Lacking the objective measuring means of prior generations, where war was often the ultimate test, we have turned to more subjective appraisal. Courage also represents to us a universal criterion of measurement, because every man would seem to have the opportunity to show courage. But talk of courage provides us with a vicarious thrill as well. It offers us the opportunity to experience excitement secondhand, the chance to put ourselves in the shoes of the man with courage.

Talking about courage often has a "Can you top this?" quality to it. But not always. Sometimes we talk about the courage of other men because it is the best way we know to show respect. Yet we're not sure what courage is and how we can distinguish it from mere showmanship. Figuring out the difference between the facade of courage and the real thing is crucial to the development of manhood and no simpler than the act of courage itself. But "understanding [particularly in relation to courage] is the wellspring of life" (Prov. 16:22).

*Taking Risks*

Some of the early risks we take stand out the most, perhaps because we were innocent at the time. It was that way for me.

When I was thirteen, I discovered that I had a choice to make about my teen years. I decided I wanted to be different. Since I was Jewish, being different meant attending a Jesuit high school. With the help of my eighth grade guidance counselor, I was able to convince my parents that this enrollment was the best thing for me to do. The actual reasons I presented to my parents escape me now. I really just wanted to go to a different town and try something different. I was looking for something foreign and new. That's indeed what I found, but it was something far greater than I was prepared for.

I didn't just want a challenge; I needed one. Intuitively I must have felt the need for a kind of growth, perhaps spiritual growth, that required a radical change of scenery. I was not that philosophical back then. At that time, the religious differences seemed a secondary consideration. I was just curious about this prep school that I had heard so much about. Religion was not in the forefront of my thoughts.

That changed during the first five minutes of the first homeroom period and continued every day of the next four years. I must have been shaking inwardly when the class got up to recite the morning prayer for the first time. The crucifixes adorning each classroom were constant reminders of my essential aloneness in this Catholic setting. As one of the first Jewish students at the high school, I had no one to turn to for comfort and guidance. I often wondered in the early days at Fairfield Prep how I was going to deal with my choice. I yearned for relief from my anxiety and I needed the promise of old: "Fear ye not, stand still, and see" (Exod. 14:13, KJV).

Being a daredevilish adolescent, I elected the path of greatest resistance. For me, such a path was to go demonstratively public in this Catholic high school. Wise convention would have dictated an alternative pathway, one in which I minded my own religious and social business. Perhaps I was too young and naive to worry, though I do remember experiencing a lot of fear as I developed a high profile in the school.

With more than mild apprehension, I chose to run for class office of vice president in my freshman year. I was realistic enough to know that the presidency was unreachable, having been set aside for those with brothers in the school and ready-made friends on the faculty. But the vice presidency seemed like the next best thing, so I went after it with all my heart, and God was "the strength of my heart" (Ps. 73:26).

I recall that my religious background was something of a central issue and a novelty during the campaign. If there were a few students who were unaware of my religious difference, they certainly were a small and invisible minority. Everyone seemed to have a question or comment about my Jewishness. If I had never fully empathized with the notion of minority status before, I could then. I campaigned on every other issue I could think about—the archaic dress code, coeducation, free periods—but nothing else seemed to matter. I was placed on center stage because of my religion.

The true day of reckoning was not election day itself but the day of platform speeches that preceded it. Into the school's age-old cafeteria/auditorium marched the class of two hundred. I didn't realize that two hundred people could make that much of a clamor, but two hundred thirteen-year-olds are capable of *Guinness Book* feats. The noise only served to heighten the tension I felt as I stepped to the platform to speak.

That day a part of me performed while another watched in disbelief. I delivered my oratory with forcefulness and confidence. I was even more perplexed when I discussed the religious issue head-on and tried to turn it to my advantage. Perhaps the most memorable moment came when I addressed the subject of religious tolerance itself, and was warmly received by the other students. The words of Moses echoed through time: "Be courageous. For the Lord your God will be with you. He will neither fail you nor forsake you" (Deut. 31:6).

The audience's response was as vociferous as it was surprising, giving me some meaningful if only introductory level of acceptance. It felt as if I had won some important contest, even if the student election was still a day away. At least everyone knew who I was, and I could truly begin to feel a part of the school. And I seemed to be bringing out the best in the people around me, too.

Then, as if riding the crest of a spiritual tidal wave, I won the vice presidential election. It was more than a dream come true; it was absolutely shocking. I felt a kind of wonderment that I still can rekindle and treasure. Perhaps just as remarkably, I was soon asked to deliver a speech to prospective prep parents about "The Benefits of a Catholic Education." A stranger, more ironic spokesperson could not be found. When you consider my interest in writing about religion, I'm not sure my life has been quite the same since.

Still, one incessant question lingers. Was it really courage that drove me to attend a traditional Catholic school and run for class officer, or was it something altogether different such as fate or circumstance or foolhardiness? That experience at age thirteen and the memorable education I received at Fairfield Prep made me consider issues of courage and determination early on. I remain fascinated by themes of courage and its possible spiritual roots.

*Facsimiles of Courage*

Like most teenagers, I never thought of my own life and circumstances in terms of courage. Courage was what appeared in the movies, and to a lesser extent, on television. It was graphic and unmistakable. That's the kind of courage that we first learn about. Unfortunately, that limited view of courage tends to stay with us as we get older. Celluloid courage gets into our bloodstream; it's a part of us that must be dealt with if we are to understand courage.

Male heroes in popular movies impose some very definite ideas about courage upon our psyches. They gain the attention of boys through their sheer force and the apparent strength of their will. Stallone, Eastwood, Bronson—all are significant contributors to American folklore and to the ever-evolving media portrayal of men. They profoundly influence our images of masculinity.

Bonded together by the similarity of their roles, such popular figures shape masculine ideals about courage by presenting themselves as models of it. They may be, on occasion, as significant in the understanding of courage as the real men in our lives. In his book *A Man's World* author Perry Garfinkel concluded: "In a society in which actual mentors are few and far between, in an age when the mythological figures that once inspired and guided us are fewer and farther, men have come to rely upon movie heroes."

Many of the largest box office successes involve the display of male courage. In motion picture after motion picture, a decidedly masculine and conspicuously similar form of courage appears. In *Rambo, Conan,* and the *Indiana Jones* series, central male characters set off on a journey in order to show their courage and tenacity. The courage is typically very literal and concrete, and the adversary is usually clear and tangible. Always, the lead male has tremendous courage. But is that realistic?

Richard Schickel, a *Time* magazine movie reviewer, has written convincingly and insightfully about the modern male lead. He was particularly sensitive to the effects that action movies might have on boys and young men. With regard to other viewers' perspectives, Schickel explained: "We, the

audience, are given the impression that they, the protagonists, know more about masculinity and courage in the end
than they actually do upon close examination."

In other words, movies often create an illusion of a
deeper form of courage than they actually depict. Ordinarily
the masculine trials and tribulations of a Clint Eastwood or
Sylvester Stallone are not full of self-examination or courageous development. The main characters are just not that
self-aware. Spiritual depth and psychological sophistication
are just not evident. "Typically, American male movie characters have been rural and earthy," noted Schickel. "They're
not forthcoming verbally. They're movers, they kick others
around." In most modern movies, dominance is the absolute
evidence of courage and the criterion by which men are
judged.

Today, actors portray masculine valor in stark, blatant,
and one-dimensional terms. If we are to believe what we see
on the silver screen, the best way for a man to demonstrate
courage is physically, by incinerating a foreign village or by
wreaking revenge on a mobster. Bravado means physical
action without hesitation or reflection; there's nothing subtle
about it.

With the priority given to graphic physical courage, movies and popular cultural heroes rarely display less obvious
forms of courage.

"Courage is rarely emotional anymore in movies," actor
Peter Naylor commented. "Our emphasis on the visual limits our portrayal of men and feeds into the cultural stereotype
of 'grin and bear it' characters. Valor is depicted the same
across most movies. If Eastwood shows no fear of death, then
it's important that Stallone not show trepidation either."

As Naylor explained, the physical courage of male

protagonists is accompanied by a conspicuous absence of fear. No building or terrain is so formidable or so impenetrable that it is beyond the mastery of these courageous demigods. The movies also suggest that no villain is so tough that he cannot be captured and destroyed, and no woman is so elusive that she cannot be won over. Most moviemakers would have us believe, that with physical courage anything is possible, and Herculean tasks are even likely. According to modern movies, physical courage makes Arnold Schwarzeneggers of us all.

With masculine prowess in the movies defined as physically facing life's challenges, we are likely to believe that courage and physical risk-taking are synonymous. We might also conclude that fear is antithetical to courage. Movies tell us that to be afraid is to be cowardly; the absence of fear is courage. Following this line of thought, we might fail to consider whether courage involves responsibility and choices in the midst of fear. But that's too "heady" an idea for many modern movies. And if we go along with the first notion, that fear is the opposite of courage, then we are inclined to deny our fears even when they are evident.

Thus, the fantasy world of movies limits our perception of courage, blinding us to its gentler side and keeping us from seeing a courage that admits mistakes and dares to be different. But such courage is real courage, a genuine ability given to us by God. "God hath not given us the spirit of fear; but of power, and of love, and of a sound mind" (2 Tim. 1:7).

We grow up with a fantasy rather than a realistic image of men. How few movies we see about the courage of an elderly man or the courage of man in relation to his children. We don't even learn about the courage within, the particular quality that makes each of us unique. Movies, television, and popular culture may try to offer facsimiles of life, but sometimes they obscure reality and fail to present the masculine soul as it truly is. Unable to adequately address religious concerns and God's role in a man's life, they implicitly deny the import of the spiritual dimension and its message: "God is our refuge and our strength" (Ps. 46:1).

*Moral Courage*

The quality that is so difficult for movies to portray is moral courage. This involves a moral choice, not just a formidable physical risk. Such a choice affects a person's total life.

In addition to their proclivity for superficial treatment of spiritual issues, many movies and television shows cannot capture moral courage because we in the greater society are also confused about what such courage is. In part, cinema reflects our perplexity about moral courage and about its masculine version.

"I used to think I knew what being a hero was. Straight and simple. I didn't mean the John Wayne stuff, but like a buddy of mine who saved a kid from a fire," remembered Alan, a forty-five-year-old journalist. "I still think that was courage, but in a lot of cases, it's hard to tell anymore. The Reagan ideals didn't wash once we got wind of the Iran arms sale," Alan lamented in conclusion.

Perhaps it requires a certain degree of courage to admit we are not certain what true courage is. But determining the essence of courage is important because it provides us with a compass with which to live, an indication of what to value in a world where values often seem diffuse and indiscernible.

We are confused when courage demands taking action or when it requires abstaining from action. In hostage crises or similar situations, we are endlessly debating the pros and cons of intervention. We find numerous parallels in business and professional circumstances, or even in our friendships and relationships. Doesn't it take greater courage to wait on a decision? We obsessively toss around the possibilities in our minds.

"To really move up in the world, a man—or a woman these days—needs to think on his feet and be able to make a decision or reach a conclusion without hesitation," concluded one interviewee named Dennis, a thirty-two-year-old real estate agent. "The old cliché that time is money is usually true. Generally, it's better to make a decision, even if it's not the best, than sit by passively and let things ride."

Although some of us would not agree with Dennis in principle, many of us follow the line of action that Dennis prescribed. We would rather be active than wait patiently. We associate "guts" with taking a firm, active stance. But impulsive actions are not always correct. Sometimes the hardest and the most courageous thing to do is wait. It's difficult to hold steady because waiting depends upon faith and the ability to be patient. It requires the courage to let go of the controls, something we men are habitually reluctant to do. "Don't be impatient. Wait for the Lord and He will come and save you! Be brave, stouthearted and courageous. Yes, wait and He will help you" (Ps. 27:14).

Discomfort with passivity flaws many men because it interferes with their capacity for moral courage. We love physical courage and illustrations of physical courage because they often involve no waiting. Passivity is anathema to most fictitious screen heroes. But it's unappealing to most of us, too. Waiting makes us anxious, and we have difficulty tolerating that anxiety. What if the desired business deal or the social meeting never takes place? How will we feel if we don't try to make them happen? That's what makes us nervous.

In fact, moral courage has a lot to do with the ability to cope with anxiety. It's the ultimate challenge that underlies most of our adult lives. The most successful and fulfilled men probably have had to encounter great anxiety in their lives, but they managed to master that anxiety. These men can appreciate pressure, weigh the risks, and wisely take charge of an ambiguous situation. These men have the courage to experience uncertainty in life and do not need facile and ready-made ways of living.

John, a forty-eight-year-old entrepreneur, seemed to me to be a man of considerable moral courage. His father died when he was fifteen. John helped put himself through college by working painstakingly throughout. As a young man, John began his own business and has since seen that business flourish through reasonable risks and excellent foresight. John is now busy setting up a small financial nest for his two sons to protect them against what happened to him when he was fifteen. It is not just this history that gives me the impression that John is a man of courage; it is also the way he speaks.

"I tell my sons, Robbie and Jeff, that it's fine to have role models and men you look up to," John explained. "But I also tell them that the things they see on television and in the newspapers, like in the sports sections, are about games and artificial events. Life is more complicated than that, and not as clear-cut. It is not just a matter of swinging for the fences. You have to learn patience and you have to know when to try something new. Nothing is permanent, except your belief in yourself and in your convictions. I tell them to have the confidence to stick to that."

*Seeing Courage Clearly*

In a sense, any man's life is a quest to understand and to integrate courage into his own world. To find courage in yourself is a soul challenge of the first order. You can spend all your life forming opinions about the courage of others, but when all is said and done, it's your own view of personal valor that really matters.

For me, through recollections and conversations with other men, a working definition of courage has begun to emerge.

Courage is a choice a person has in the face of formidable and consequential events. Those circumstances can range from moving to marriage, but courage is one option a person has in reaction to the event. The form of courage may be physical, intellectual, or emotional, though a blend of the three may result in the deepest kind of courage. Courage that involves all of these qualities is nearly always courage expressed in real-life circumstances, not in games or play.

Courage is also the means by which a man's dedication to his ideals is tested. It is relatively easier to adhere to your ideals when little or no risk is involved. But when I risk something important, like popularity or the endearment of others, which is important to many men, then it requires courage to listen to the beat of my own soul. Sometimes God seems to be my only ally; but "the Lord is the strength of my life; of whom shall I be afraid?" (Ps. 27:1)

My high school experience was a watershed in my spiritual development, a fortunate discovery more than an indisputable act of courage. But there is one thing that I remain very proud of. Once I had begun to speak up, I didn't allow the doubting words of others at school or the concerns of my family to deter me. I saw an appointed spiritual task before me, and I prepared myself for the challenge of running for office. Given that I was thirteen at the time, that spiritual act called for a form of courage I can still respect today.

Courage reveals our choices, tests our ideals, and challenges our independence of spirit. Courage is a soulfulness fresh and unique for each individual man. I believe in that spirit. The more men with whom I have spoken, the more I have come to appreciate individual variations on the theme of courage. Every man displays courage with his own style and grace. For the politician, it may come in the form of a new policy or political position. For the fireman, it may be the gritty way he protects the community. No matter. Men stick their necks out and make a difference in the world, and God is always there guiding their path.

Perseverance is a frequent companion to courage. It is rare to find a meaningful act of courage that wasn't preceded by forethought and determination. The courageous man doesn't give up easily, but he does know when giving up makes sense. That relinquishing of effort can be a gutsy act in itself. But soulful courage can include both perseverance and letting go, and it takes flexibility to do both. For example, when you're part of a team at work, you may work diligently yourself, but you must also trust in the fine labor of others.

The independent and persevering spirit makes choices and stands for ideals, but this spirit is also willing to wait. Increasingly in a fast-paced society such as ours, the courage to delay rewards and gratification has become more scarce. But it is a valuable form of courage. The greatest rewards, like the fulfillment of the masculine self, require a long-term commitment. That's a form of courage that all of us can benefit from.

What is your preferred form of courage? What kind of risks do you take? The answers to those two questions can tell you a great deal about your relationship to your soul. Soulfulness requires courage, but it may not call for conventional courage. Your particular form of courage may go unnoticed to the outside observer. But you know what makes you who you are, so recognize your own expressions of valor. You are one of those men who, as much as the decorated military man or the celebrated athlete, have a right to be called gutsy. So accept your own courage.

In discovering your own sense of courage, you will also encounter God, for He is the inspiration behind meaningful courage. God is there for us when we reach deeply into ourselves to summon courage. God has helped me in my life to deal with my fears, not avoid or deny them. He can help you in yours, too. As the well-known passage from Psalms poetically reveals: "Even when walking through the dark valley of death I will not be afraid, for you are close beside me, guarding, guiding all the way" (Ps. 23:4).

# CHAPTER 4

# IN SEARCH OF
# TRUTH

**A** few years ago I was sitting at the kitchen table of my parents' house in Connecticut, alone with my father. We sat there silently. On the table lay a set of family dolls, six miniature persons collected for my studies with children. I've seen many youngsters and adults arrange these dolls, both for research and for fun. I have seen children of divorced parents separate the mother and father dolls, and I have observed children of a deceased parent lay aside one doll or the other in an inactive, reclining position. When I glanced out the window to look at the snow for a moment, the dolls were routinely scattered on the table. When I looked back, I saw to my profound anguish that my father had done something with the dolls that I had never seen before. He had piled the little figures in an awful tangled heap, their delicate bodies thrown about like so many scraps of human carnage. I felt my heart and my stomach drop. There was a sad, plaintive look on my father's face. My father is a Holocaust survivor. The dolls that lay before us embodied how his mother and father and sisters died. In that moment I was privy to his memories. They became mine, too.

The Holocaust was my father's reality, and indirectly mine as well. Through my father, and through the heart-breaking experiences of his life, I have learned that a man must deal with his life circumstances—no matter how frankly painful and overwhelming they might seem. Not to accept even the harshest of realities, or to cover them up with denial or distortion, is to live falsely. For an individual to be authentic, he must stay true to his experiences. "Never forget who you are," my father has always said to me. This same principle applies to the lives of individual men, but it is also true of nations and of men collectively. Without a sense of truth about who we are and what we represent, there can be no genuine sense of personal or national integrity. "He who walks with integrity walks securely" (Prov. 10:9).

### A Tale of Two Leaders

During the spring of 1983, my father and I attended the first "Gathering of American Holocaust Survivors" in Washington, D.C. The conference was the largest reunion of survivors in this country to date. Some ten thousand Nazi victims assembled in the nation's capital to recall their shared past and make sense out of their common anguish. They were there to bear witness. The reality of their collective experiences was somber indeed, nearly unimaginable to any reasonable person. But this cruel piece of history, experienced so tragically and personally by these survivors, beckoned to be remembered.

The most compelling thing about the gathering was not the sights and sounds but the silence. It was a deep and restless silence. It was a silence that befitted the reopening of six million graves. A common sight during the four-day conference was a dozen survivors huddled around a gray table—saying nothing to each other, but sharing the moment as if it contained some hidden meaning. There was also a computer search for lost relatives, which for nearly all survivors was a search in vain. A lifetime of tension filled the air as each survivor stepped forward to the "Search Table." Each face, including my father's trembling one, was marked by fragmentary hope and sadness. No one to find. Just memories. All that was left was for each survivor to record his or her story. So we pressed on to the "History Table," where a patient man with a tape recorder heard the accounts of horror with the ears of a saint. My father related the sorrow of his life with an incessant drive to remember all details, each lonely morsel transmitted with a cracking voice. I will never forget his voice that day. His heart remembered what his mind forgot. And so it was for all the ten thousand survivors assembled in Washington; their hearts were deep (Ps. 64:6, KJV).

The formal climax of the gathering was a commemoration held at the Capital Center. This was to be the official decree of a national remembrance. The speakers were President Reagan and Professor Elie Wiesel, the widely acclaimed poet of the Holocaust and Nobel Prize recipient. I recall the murmur of the crowd in anticipation. It was a scene filled with passions and memories, a particularly ironic scene for a collection of persons so painfully sensitive to crowds and rallies and vocal political figures.

When survivor Elie Wiesel rose to address the crowd, he appeared as an unimposing, down-to-earth figure grateful for an opportunity to speak with his peers. He was slight and unassuming, far from the stereotypical American male mold. As he spoke, he seemed refreshingly free of an ego and concerns about his performance. He talked about the historical and cultural significance of the Holocaust, as well as the meaning of the catastrophe for all men. But he also tackled the spiritual questions that echo years after the Holocaust, questions about faith and doubt and the nature of man's propensity for good and evil. As a man reverberating with such pain and sensitivity that you felt that you were on the podium with him, Wiesel struggled with the ineffability and the frank absurdity of what he had experienced. He seemed to unveil his own inner life before the eyes and ears of those in attendance. He was clearly waging a spiritual battle in search of the truth. And he was giving of himself genuinely and generously in that pursuit.

President Reagan's appearance was strikingly different. Great pomp and circumstance accompanied his entrance, as at any other official event. But that entrance set the tone, for President Reagan went about this speech as just another function of his office. In contrast to Wiesel's solemnity, Reagan was upbeat and aggressive. There was an air of performance and theatrics as he spoke, and a sense of a subtler motive behind his spoken agenda. He spoke of the Soviet Union and past atrocities there, but his points seemed to miss their mark. He seemed to be using the conference to further his own geopolitical policies, rather than reach out to the survivors or grapple with the lessons of the Holocaust. He presented no cogent view of history nor any apparent effort at understanding. Perhaps what was most disturbing was the simplistic way in which President Reagan discussed the Holocaust. Against a backdrop of profound human anguish and complex theological questions, in which all major religions were represented, President Reagan's words were full of avoidance and personal distance. Lamentably, he could not embrace the reality of the Holocaust.

It was a dramatic study in contrast between two men and a scenario that would soon reemerge with the infamous Bitburg incident. Bitburg was the site of a German cemetery that President Reagan visited during a trip to West Germany. It was not just an ordinary burial ground but a military one, and there he joined West German leaders in commemorating the Nazi war dead. The event immediately became a source of international controversy and embarrassment, as President Reagan seemed to display a callous disregard for history. Moreover, his decision to participate appeared inauthentic, quite possibly a choice born of political expediency rather than conscience. In the days following the incident, Elie Wiesel became one of President Reagan's most outspoken critics. In a very tense exchange at the White House, Wiesel characteristically shared the contents of his heart.

"Mr. President," Wiesel said respectfully, "your place is not there [Bitburg]. Your place is with the *victims* [of the Holocaust]."

As the survivors' memorable gathering in Washington had foreshadowed, the Bitburg speech and resulting controversy are now a small but revealing part of American history during the Reagan years. No doubt I see such events with a special filter; I view them in light of my father's pain and experiences. But I see beyond that personal meaning to the greater lessons involved. I often think of the events surrounding Reagan and Wiesel, one the epitome of a popular contemporary image of masculinity and the other a symbol of the conscience of the twentieth century. They serve as reminders to me of the paramount place of truthfulness and authenticity in human affairs. It is vital for leaders, but it is equally crucial for any man. Like true leaders, real men are genuine; they are straightforward, sincere, in touch with themselves and with the passage of events, both personal and historical. A real man listens to the special ticking of his own heart, but he also weighs that against past experience and the good of others.

I have found that men do care deeply about being true to themselves. A sense of personal honesty is intrinsic to the character of a man at peace. For men like my father and Elie Wiesel, survivors of inordinate trauma, facing the reality of their experience is an awesome task. But for the rest of us, our national leaders included, capturing the truth in our own lives is no simple matter either. There is no blueprint for authenticity. Guided by history and the lessons of other men before us, each of us must find his own authenticity. That's what it means to be a real man. "A good man is known by his truthfulness" (Prov. 12:17).

### Child of a Survivor

I don't know if I see everything through the lens of the Holocaust or through my particular vantage point as the child of a survivor. I am certain, however, that I see some important aspects of masculinity from that perspective.

I define authenticity in a particular way. I see authenticity as not only being true to your convictions but being true to

God as well. The Holocaust teaches that a person can be true to his convictions and still commit heinous crimes, if his convictions are misguided. Therefore, I believe that the authentic man is true to his own heart—yet he also makes certain that his heart is aligned with the goodness of God.

The knowledge of my background compels me to search for honesty in the world and in my everyday existence. Such realism is essential for me to cope with my heritage; it helps me and others around me to properly learn from the Holocaust and serve God with reverence.

How is the male child of a survivor different from other men when it comes to issues of manhood? First, he is born into pain. From the womb, he knows that suffering is as much a part of his family's history as religion or politics is for other people. He becomes aware early on that his culture has faced a threat of epic proportions. If several battles had ended differently during World War II, cultural annihilation would have been likely. How can he respond as a man to this legacy? Even as he tries to run from the Holocaust's awful embrace, he can never escape the inevitable feeling that it has profoundly shaped who he is. His very existence stands as an exception to the millions who were its victims. The cultural pathos is overwhelming. But in the privacy of his own soul, where he must weld his own sense of manhood, he must pursue his own individual answers.

What else does the Holocaust teach to those so closely affected by it and to the rest of the world? It reminds us of what can happen if men go horribly astray from their basic nature. It teaches us that humanity and decency must be constantly protected or we all suffer as men. In relation to those countries and individuals who knew what was happening in Eastern Europe and nevertheless remained silent, the Holocaust suggests that passive complacency and indifference can be as much a failure of character as genocide itself. Real men stand up against atrocity even if it doesn't seem to involve them directly. Whether it is senseless war in a distant corner of the globe or an injustice in the neighborhood, whether it's the Jewish Holocaust or the Cambodian Holocaust or the massacre of students in China, it is important to rise up and take a stance. Authenticity requires that a man express his outrage at evil and destruction. No man should be neutral when other men are being mistreated and abused. We must ask ourselves, "Can I discern between good and evil?" (2 Sam. 19:35, KJV).

Lamentably, I have also learned from the Holocaust that even authentic behavior does not guarantee happiness or even survival. Many good people, steadfastly adhering to their values, died tragically in the inferno and in the larger war that surrounded it. In that sense, my father was fortunate; he didn't die, although he was emotionally wounded for life. The absurdity and unfairness of the Holocaust weigh heavily on his mind today as much as yesterday.

Like my father, I cannot escape its shadow either. Yet I know in my heart that an authentic life is the only fitting response to the Holocaust. In the face of apparent absurdity, it is vital to stand for meaningfulness in life. I find that I have a tremendous need to make my days meaningful, and trying to be true to myself and to God is the best course. Telling the truth gives me "great satisfaction" (Prov. 12:14).

Holocaust survivor and author Viktor Frankl wrote that the real challenge of the Holocaust is to make meaning out of the chaos, to continue to hope. For an individual man, that means sticking to his beliefs and ideals even when they appear shattered. That is a philosophy I try to live by. I find no alternative. To attempt a different route, a circuitous path toward success or freedom, will only lead a man away from himself and from God as well. Even in the midst of personal turmoil, believing in yourself makes a statement louder than the turmoil itself, even if it is heard only after you're gone. That is one of the undeniable messages that comes out of the tears and anguish of the Holocaust.

Not all the lessons of history's darkest hour are so esoteric or philosophical. The event continues to influence me in countless pragmatic ways as well. As a writer, I know that the Holocaust is part of my background, and I feel moved to reflect that in my work. But the Holocaust as a topic can be very consuming, and I do not wish to be consumed by it, so utterly immersed in it that I lose sight of the flowers and the trees around. It is possible to work too close to the flames.

I am finding that I can most meaningfully contribute by applying my background to the study of religion, culture, and the nature of men. It is no mere coincidence that I have become intrigued by questions of men and spirituality, and men and their relationship to God. A knowledge of the Holocaust causes me to explore these subjects with an undivided heart. Even if I occasionally become disheartened, I sense that these topics are important in making a better understanding among men. Although the Holocaust may be a source of great pain for my father and me, it points out the direction our lives must follow, and in an ironic way reassures us that the Lord is our "salvation" (2 Sam. 22:19).

*What Men Have to Say About Being a Real Man*

From my background as a child of a survivor and from other personal observations, I have formed a reasonably clear definition of manhood. But I recognize the dangers of too narrow or fixed a notion of manhood. That is one reason I'm intrigued by what other men of vastly different backgrounds have to say about the subject. Learning about the ideas of other men, particularly those whose experiences contrast with mine, helps to expand my views and sometimes my sense of manhood as well.

Over the last few years, I have asked a number of men to talk about what makes a man. In seeking out friends, colleagues, and random persons to interview, I have tried to find men who come from diverse settings and whose life experiences might be quite a bit different from mine. I have asked dozens of men to offer their definition of "a real man." I did not begin with high expectations about their responses, nor did I start with a formal hypothesis, just a curiosity about what men would say when they discussed the subject in a serious manner.

What I discovered in my ad hoc survey was that men responded in a number of recognizable ways about masculinity. I found myself able to relate to most of their ideas. At the same time, I noticed that the theme of honesty—either in relation to the self or others—did not emerge with any regularity. That omission surprised me. Five characteristics were commonly highlighted by men in their descriptions of real men. These qualities were toughness, intelligence, a calm sense of control, raw individualism, and a modern sensitivity to changing times.

*Toughness.* Some of the men I questioned felt that real

men were identified by a hard-driving and persistent toughness. They saw the attainment of manhood as both a goal and a statement of existence, a rite that must be continuously earned through grit and strength. They thought that real men were older, more experienced, and time-tested. In their view, a real man was someone who had been dramatically challenged by war, injury, misfortune, or some ordeal and who had triumphed over his demanding physical test.

Wayne, a thirty-eight-year-old fireman, was one man who saw masculinity in this way. Although Wayne's comments may have been greatly colored by the two years he spent in Vietnam, he spoke for many other men who have never been in the armed forces.

"Men have to know what life is all about. You have to be aware of what's going on in the world. And you have to know how life works. You shouldn't need to be smacked over the head with a hammer to realize that life is tough. Nobody gives you anything. You have to earn it. You have to take life for all that you can. There are no guarantees. As a fireman I see an awful lot," Wayne concluded, "and it makes you bounce back when things aren't going your way. Keeps you from feeling sorry for yourself and being soft."

But is the essence of manhood a matter of toughness and savvy about life alone, as Wayne implied? Given my father's background, I have wondered about that. Is surviving in the world enough? Many other men didn't think so.

*Intellect.* Some perceived manhood as an intellectual quality and saw themselves as thinking craftsmen, with the ability to see life in nuances and make decisions accordingly. They described a real man as being bright, clever, and opportunistic. Some even suggested that a man can be manipulative if he has a good rationale for it. Manipulation could be okay if he stayed within the boundaries of law and reason. According to this view, if manhood were only a matter of physical strength and tenacity, we would still be cavemen. Being a civilized man requires foresight and mental acumen. When it comes to world problems, such as superpower relations, these men were quite optimistic that reason will overcome all tensions.

Twenty-nine-year-old Rob, a medical school student, illustrates a man who sees masculinity in intellectual terms. Rob was outspoken and even verbose at times about his notions of manhood.

Rob began by telling me that he welcomed the opportunity to discuss this subject. He quickly launched into a monologue: "I've done a good amount of thinking about the concept of a real man. Would you call it a concept or a myth? A lot of women friends I have say that they are more attracted to a man by the way he thinks rather than how he looks or how much he can bench-press. I am sure that's how most people under forty feel today. You have to look at it sociologically. The proving grounds and the rites of passage for men these days are in business, law, or some other cerebral profession—all avenues for intelligence, not brawn!"

Rob concealed some of his view of men, but others were more direct. They found mental activity and intellectual careers were the best ways to release aggression. Having found no physical outlet or other satisfactory resolution, they channeled aggression into shrewdness and cunning. As one of Rob's cohorts, a like-minded thirty-three-year-old fellow, put it: "Men can think on their feet; of course, thinking on your feet can mean learning how to be shifty with your feet!"

*Control.* A third wave of men was taken aback by this portrait of real men as opportunistic. They didn't see themselves as shifting with the rising tide of circumstances at all. They viewed themselves as more solid and firm. In fact, they believed that men should be characterized by calm resolve and unshaken purpose. In their way of looking at things, any problem or situation was best addressed by "sticking to your guns." These individuals stressed that men must control their emotions and not be overcome by anxiety, regardless of the consequences. They pinpointed this quality as important for world or national leaders. Finally, these men had a subtle way of discounting men who were not like themselves, perhaps out of the need to reinforce the male status quo.

"Real men are those guys who can be calm under fire," asserted forty-five-year-old Tom, a pilot. "One example that occurs to me—I guess I'm thinking about it because I saw a movie about Pearl Harbor last week—is Roosevelt with the Japanese. He really took charge of the situation. Men do that. They are not quick to panic if something goes wrong. And they don't do things like trade arms for hostages just because they are frustrated, either. You cannot let your emotions dictate decisions. Whatever kind of job you have, I don't care if it's president or night watchman, you have to have a steady pulse and good judgment."

Whereas men like Tom espoused a conventional view of authentic manhood and additionally stressed the interrelationships among men, other men accepted some of their values about emotion and judgment but emphasized individualism. These men uplifted those who accomplished a great deal without outside assistance. Indeed, self-reliance became almost a religious tenet for them.

*Individualism.* Is a real man a self-sufficient individual? Although not all the men who affirmed self-sufficiency could describe themselves that way, they all admired the independent man. They seemed to define self-sufficiency as the absence of a need for others' emotional support and guidance. They felt that self-sufficiency was requisite for a man to demonstrate prowess in his own right. Whether the purpose was surpassing other men or simply moving forward in their lives, these men treasured singular courage and risk taking.

As they talked about manhood, these respondents conveyed a sense of drivenness. Their standards for manhood were often more extreme than those of other men, and they frequently saw manhood as something that only a few chosen men could attain. In contrast, the Bible declares, "we have access by faith" (Rom. 5:2, KJV).

"I most admire a guy like Chuck Yeager, the fellow who broke the sound barrier," asserted forty-three-year old Carl, an elevator repairman. "Not only because he dared to do what nobody else had the guts to, but because of the quiet, confident way that apparently he went about it. It really seemed like he was his own man. From what I understand, he didn't really get that much help. It was too bad he got a raw deal when they were picking the first astronauts. But maybe the 'yessir' stuff wasn't for him."

After Carl talked so emphatically about Chuck Yeager, he decided in a moment to offer another observation: "Ralph Nader, the consumer crusader, is another guy I like, because he doesn't care about what anybody in big business thinks. He'd go after GM if he believed that he had a case. Sometimes he seems like a loner, but he is doing something that needs to be done. He's protecting the little guy. He has his own little task force or whatever you call it, and that way he stays clean of any outside influence."

*Modern Sensitivity.* Although such views of heroic figures who do it alone have been part of the American landscape for some time, a fifth perspective on the real man is less entrenched. Found more often among younger men, the notion of a sensitive male has now become a convention for modern times in its own right. Some of these younger men see real men as more passionate and sensitive than their older predecessors, particularly in relation to the needs of women. What is not clear is whether these qualities that are prized, such as openness and empathy, are mere surface changes or actually enduring developments in the male character.

Men who stressed sensitivity were much less likely to use words like "grit" and "guts" in describing an ideal man. Their ideas were less fixed and less clear at times. It was often hard for them to define what sensitivity was, even though they used it freely in their depictions. They seemed more comfortable with passive roles and uncertainty than most other men. They accepted the notion of a real man to a certain extent, but always related their ideas to women.

"I'm not sure if I believe that there is such a thing as a real man, at least in the way it is usually meant. I don't like bravado and showing off, the jock mentality. But I guess I do believe that you can be a real man by being emotional and aware of other people's needs. Men should realize that people are people and that women are people, too. Most of us have mistreated women for too long. Things have not changed all that much, but I try to do the little I can," finished Chris, a thirty-year-old insurance agent.

When I asked Chris if he could paint a picture of what men should be like, he paused for a while and seemed befuddled. It seemed that he was more certain about what men should *not* be like than how they should act. "I guess a man should be aware of changing times, and not just act the way his father did," Chris concluded.

Included in these five different views of manhood are many interesting and worthwhile qualities. The men admired characteristics that, in some cases, could lead to a more satisfying life. Yet I was also interested in what they didn't say. These men found it difficult to address just being themselves. At least for the purposes of my interview with them, the men anchored themselves with views from the popular culture. The idea of being yourself was sometimes, though not always, lost in the acquired imagery of maleness. Few men answered my questions in very personal ways; the theme of authenticity did not come up very often even in an abstract sense. What these men did not reveal concerns me and makes me believe that we must put a more active effort into discovering what makes each of us unique.

### How Can We Be More Authentic?

Many of us spend our lives traveling in the wrong direction, searching in vain for a secure manhood. We want very much to label ourselves as "real men" or call ourselves whatever the current phrase may be. Unfortunately, we are too slow to realize that authenticity is the best way to respect ourselves and appreciate other men as well. "The Lord's path is truth" (Ps. 25:10).

Authenticity is the secret destination in life for all of us, but so few of us are aware of that. We must allow self-truth into our lives so that it can affect the way we think and act. Why? Because authenticity is so much a part of manhood that no real manhood exists without it. How? By asking ourselves in business and social and personal situations: "Am I being genuine?" "Is my heart in the right place?" "Am I dedicated to the truth?"

One reason men may neglect authenticity is that it is

complex; it doesn't openly display itself like courage or passion. It almost seems invisible. But it does exist. Authenticity requires the ability to discriminate between what is true and good for the self from what is not. Making the best choices in life requires a tireless dedication to authenticity, an awareness of what best fits us. Only honesty about ourselves can sustain us over time. Truth will stand "the test of time" (Prov. 12:19).

A second reason men bypass authenticity is that society sometimes puts obstacles and distractions in our path. How can we find our real beliefs when we are bombarded with trivial information? Technology and the hurried pace of our society have robbed us of the time required for soul-searching. In frustration, many men give up the quest for authenticity altogether.

Nevertheless, persistence pays when it comes to inner development. If authentic behavior doesn't in itself make the world a better place, then at least it increases the chances for that to occur. Every man's dedication to truth can make a difference. By being true to ourselves, we will also refresh others "like water from a mountain spring" (Prov. 13:14).

We must first start with what is closest to home. To become more authentic, we must turn away from showmanship and bravado and replace these with substance and sincerity. That means acting as we really feel, not in accordance with what is expected by others. That demands less emphasis on surface appearances and greater emphasis on the inner person. It is better to *feel* masculine than look masculine, though the two need not be exclusive of each other. Remember that manhood is a state of mind, not a matter of appearances alone.

To walk along an authentic path toward self-discovery, a man must seriously consider his relationship to other men. We must learn the difference between independence from men and interdependence with them. Isolationism limits manhood; shared experiences broaden us. These include the development of male friendships, the emergence of camaraderie, and the opportunity to work in group situations toward a common goal. For example, if a neighbor needs to borrow some tools or equipment, we share readily for several reasons—to develop the friendship, to establish a neighborly bond, to show appreciation for our mutual need for each other, and even to beautify the neighborhood! Interdependence is vital for manhood because it is endemic to the male character. For a man to experience kinship with his friends and cohorts is simply to be true to his character.

A third cornerstone of an authentic life is respect of self. Men may neglect self-worth out of fear of excessive self-involvement. A man has an obligation to take care of himself; and the way he treats himself will eventually foreshadow how he will treat others who are close to him. So he must provide attention to his own integrity and self-esteem.

Respecting ourselves is synonymous with honoring ourselves. By respecting ourselves, each of us makes a statement of conviction: "There is something noble and worthwhile about my manliness." When we are convinced in our hearts of our worthiness, we swear an oath of realism. Each of us does indeed have an inherent honor. That does not mean we should idealize ourselves, but equally we should not cheapen or lessen ourselves. Each of us, with our own unique version of manliness, represents an important and significant human being. "But every man hath his proper gift of God" (1 Cor. 7:7, KJV).

We do not nurture authenticity as much by the words of others as by the fires of our own heart. Each man has an original spirit that is decidedly male and profoundly full of life. We must discover that spirit even if it demands great patience and energy. For a man to find himself, and therefore become a real man, he must learn to separate his fiction from his truth and live life guided by that truth.

### Where Does God Fit In?

It is possible to doubt the existence of God and still maintain that a man must be authentic. A person can hold that position and cite reasons like "the common good," "the brotherhood of man," or even "self-fulfillment" to rational- ize the need for authenticity. Yet it is not the most direct or certain way of ensuring self-honesty. For that degree of cer- tainty, belief in God is necessary.

The centered and heartfelt belief in God implicitly de- mands that a man be honest with himself. Why? Because following God means that a man also makes a commitment to follow the truth in his own life. God is the ultimate truth in a world that is often full of enigmas and contradictions, divorces, injuries, and historical traumas like the Holocaust. But only God offers a possibility of making such inexplicable events meaningful. Only His truth can be our shield (Ps. 91:4).

The clearest connection between God and truth occurs when we try to be authentic on an everyday basis. When our choices are consistent with our personalities, God is there. When our fears and distortions about ourselves have dissipated, God is the inner voice in each of us. In situations where our mettle is tested, we are relying on God when we respond with conviction and sincerity, though often we are unaware or cannot recognize God's presence. God sees us through challenging and changing times by reminding us who we are and by refreshing our memories about our values and character. Ultimately God tells us that we are men of spiritual character, and that makes our vantage point all the better in relation to an authentic life.

In practical terms, when we face troublesome and plaguing decisions at work, when we lose a friend, or when severe self-doubts creep in, responding in an authentic way to life is most critical. When problems emerge in our marriages or when we find ourselves repeatedly scolding our children, then locating a calm inner voice is most crucial. These are the times that test our souls, when we desperately need God. And God is there for us, right at the moment when we are prepared to look into the mirror of the soul. When we are ready to stand toe-to-toe with ourselves and see beyond our surface masculinity, then God is there to guide us. Just as God is central to an appreciation of authenticity, so our efforts at being genuine are essential for growing closer to God.

Because of my family legacy and also what I have learned from other men, I believe that real men are real in the sense that they are true to their spiritual destinies, in line with the will of God. Believing that God is real is the key to all truth about ourselves. The realization of God's existence in our lives makes us come to acknowledge our souls. It provides us with a base from which to get to know ourselves, as well as a spiritual compass by which to live authentically.

In pursuing God, we will inevitably follow the course of truth, not just some abstract or ethereal sense of truth, but a truth of our own—a truth that helps us understand who we are as men and what we can accomplish on earth.

# CHAPTER 5

# THE GOOD
# FIGHT OF
# FAITH

**D**uring my training to become a psychotherapist, an older supervisor often spoke to me about gender issues. So when my clients, both male and female, discussed their relationships and their marriages, I took my notes and impressions to Dr. Michael Broadman, a senior psychoanalyst, to seek his advice. Gray-haired, rotund, and nearing his sixtieth birthday, Dr. Broadman seemed an unlikely expert on contemporary men and women, but his clear wisdom consistently overcame my doubts. During my weekly meetings with Dr. Broadman, I listened with great attentiveness, eager to savor each morsel of understanding.

"David, have you ever noticed what most men who need help have in common?" Dr. Broadman asked me one afternoon somewhat out of the blue.

After I offered a naive suggestion or two, my supervisor began to answer his own question. "More often than not, men suffer from problems of faith. They lose faith too easily in themselves, in life, and in everything they believe in. They may not, we may not, admit it to ourselves, but the liveliness of faith has abandoned us. But why does this happen?"

Again I did not know what to say. I had a few ideas, but I was afraid to venture them forth. I wasn't sure where Dr. Broadman was headed.

"We lose faith," he continued, "because we are saddled by anger and we lose touch with a good deal of our inner emotional life. Many men cannot really relate to the wide variety of feelings they maintain underneath. Without access to the richness of experience, it is understandable that the world can look a little gray and bleak. Faith and hope depend upon a little light shining through in a person's life, and we need to be free of anger and be comfortable with our other emotions in order to see the light."

"Are women's problems different?" I then asked with interest.

"Not entirely," Dr. Broadman responded. "But women are somewhat more sophisticated in their acceptance of their feelings. That can provide them with more ready access to faith. But many men relate to their feelings as if their feelings were alien particles from another planet! The presence of these strange feelings would make it seem like an unsafe universe."

"How does this influence the way we help men?" I questioned.

Dr. Broadman seemed pleased with my efforts to focus the discussion. He smiled knowingly. As he leaned forward in his old easy chair, he offered this piece of guidance: "The first job you have as a good therapist is the same you have as a friend. You must introduce a fellow to the idea that all his feelings, not just his drivenness or his anger, are feelings worthy of his respect. Only then can you help him to better understand himself. Only then can you help restore his faith in the world, and even help him build on his faith. You must help a man let go of his need for control and allow his life to proceed as it should."

Dr. Broadman's insights held up for male client after male client. Yet his visions seemed even more applicable to hurting men I knew who were unable to reach out for help. In my internships, I regularly saw young boys and men whose anxiety caused them to put their feelings into action, or even worse, to close out their emotions altogether. The only identifiable feeling for some was anger. Now, several years after my training, I am convinced that this is true for many men. Faith is a great dilemma for us, complicated by our anger, but the man of faith should not be "hasty . . . to be angry" (Eccles. 7:9, KJV).

Experts frequently address the controversial relationship between men and their emotions, but they rarely point out the impact of that relationship on their outlook on life in general and religious faith in particular. Yet since faith in his world and in himself is a great pillar of his masculinity, a man needs to acknowledge the connection between his feelings and his faith.

*The Obstacle of Anger*

If it is true that no man can serve two masters, then it is not possible to harbor anger and fully embrace God at the same time. Yet anger is the one emotion that many men feel comfortable with, a passion they can safely label "manly" and rationalize as a man's privilege.

In the Book of Exodus, the people became angry and impatient with God and constructed a golden calf. Their rebellion against God grew out of their anger, a disposition that blinded their vision and overshadowed all their other emotions. The situation required Moses to act as a liaison between God and the wayward people. Consumed by anger, the people could not serve God properly.

The same is true for men today. Too often we are so tied to anger and resentment that genuine faith in life and in God is untenable. Anger stays with us, revealing its ugly nature in such guises as insensitivity to a subordinate at work, impatience with an elderly man who is driving too slowly, and failure to return a phone call because there is nothing in it for us. Anger need not be demonstrative; subtle acts of passive aggressiveness are sometimes the most painful and devastating to others.

"I've been screwed by life," a former patient of mine said matter-of-factly. The fact that he was only twenty-one years old made his comment that much more biting and sad. Clearly it was too early to sum up what life had delivered to him, but his anger persisted. "My parents didn't really care about me. My father is a doctor whose only love was work. My mother was too busy with her friends. Sure, they gave us whatever money could buy, but so what? Since I've become independent, all I find in the world is mediocrity. What's there to get out of bed in the morning for?"

"Would you prefer that I answer your question or just note that I realize that you are very angry, Tom?" I responded.

"You bet I'm angry. And I have a right to be!" Tom continued.

"I don't mean to dispute your right," I explained, "but I do mean to ask you to consider what your anger is really about and what it does for you." When I had Tom's undivided attention, I added: "Maybe we could also consider what's underneath your anger and what it may interfere with, too."

That suggestion marked the beginning of my first real communication with Tom. The questions I posed to him I have also asked myself. These questions also apply to men outside of the therapeutic setting. A man does not have to be ill or even obviously troubled to have struggles over anger. Sometimes anger just seems to be part of our collective experience. "Every man bears his own burden" (Gal. 6:5).

Anger is an acceptable emotion in the male social world. As boys, we are ordinarily encouraged to be curious, active, and aggressive. These pursuits are healthy and formative, but sometimes we're not given a sense of direction to accompany them. No other emotion is sanctioned for boys and men the way anger is. It stands alone, and sometimes it speaks for us.

What are we angry about? Many things—and religion is a significant target. First, some of us are still upset with our parents for their shortcomings. We may remain bitter at our mothers for their lack of nurturance or resent our fathers for their distance or coldness. Second, we may be angry at the outside world, which we blame for our frustrations, disappointments, and misfortunes. Third, we may blame God and/or religion for not healing our wounds or offering us enough basis for hope. This anger, whatever its origins, blocks our path to wholeness and spirituality. The size of this boulder is so massive, it is sometimes difficult to measure, and it is so familiar, we think of it as a permanent part of our landscape.

"Sometimes I just blow my top," commented fifty-five-year-old Max, a truck driver. "I don't always know why. I feel bad afterward, but I can't do anything about it. I guess it just overtakes me, sort of. Temper has always been a problem for me. Even when I was a boy, I'd fly off the handle. So much would build up inside, I had to let it out."

When religion is the subject of men's wrath, it is often the institution of religion that men complain about. Religious guidelines and practices seem too restrictive or outdated. We do not like being told what to do or how to behave. A church or synagogue looms over us like an extension of parental authority, rather than as a sanctuary of free expression. In any case, we rebel. Some of us leave religious affiliations entirely; others simply minimize their importance.

If, on the other hand, a man is angry at God, the reasons often center around God's mystery. We grow angry with God for His apparent elusiveness, invisibility, and intangibility. We refuse to chase after this enigmatic God, choosing instead to reject His teachings or even disclaim them. We resent how difficult it seems to reach God—the path seems so narrow. Our anger grows into a denial of God's existence.

More common among men is subtle or implicit anger with God. Societal taboos against pejoratively invoking God's name force our resentment to stay under the surface. We are silently at war with God. Indignant that God has not fulfilled our needs or answered all our prayers, we reject God for not being there when we need Him. In the privacy of our own thoughts, we disassociate ourselves from God through our anger.

"Don't get me wrong—I'm no atheist," volunteered forty-one-year-old Vinnie, a man of Catholic background. "It's the church I'm against. What does it do for people? What right do they have to tell grown-up men how to run their lives? Sometimes I think people are better off without religion."

Although aggressiveness is necessary for societies to progress, to build bridges and devise new conceptual strategies, anger is not. It is a divisive passion; it creates distance and antagonism between people. It distorts and dominates other experiences. Its consuming nature leaves little room for compassion, empathy, and love. Because it interferes with the tender emotions in particular, it also obstructs a man's road toward faith, a synthesis of many varied feelings and beliefs. We cannot allow emotional roadblocks because we are asked to serve God with all our hearts (Deut. 11:13, KJV).

### A Penchant for Control

Anger has a dangerous irony; it allows us to control others by losing control of ourselves. An angry man in a crowd may get his way because others fear his wrath. A belligerent father may assume the role of a dictator because he intimidates his wife and children with his overpowering physical and vocal presence. A man who loses control of himself in anger frequently gains control over his surroundings.

When a man's tendency toward anger lessens, his need for control does not necessarily disappear. More often than not, we fight desperately against the forces of growth and change—and the variety of feelings that go with them—by controlling whatever we can in our lives. Rather than permitting our days to flow naturally, we exert a great deal of effort to keep our experiences contained and muzzled, not realizing that experiences are more valuable than wealth. God teaches us through our experiences and that is a blessing we must learn to accept.

"I like to have every workday planned the day before," said Jay, a thirty-five-year-old architect. "I like to know exactly what my next project will be. That way there's no wasted time, and you can control unforeseen problems. On weekends I find myself doing the same thing, because there's no way I could get in golf or tennis if I didn't. The more control you have over your life, the better your chances are to be satisfied."

Control allows us to imagine ourselves to be masters of our own destinies. It gives us the impression that all limitations are self-imposed, making us feel efficacious, demonstrative, and even powerful. Control provides an illusion of safety from dangers like uncertainty and anxiety.

But control is not necessarily our ally. When exaggerated, it can preclude discovery of the outside world as well as ourselves. In an effort to create a fixed order to our lives, we lock ourselves into circumscribed and repetitive patterns of living. For example, Jay had difficulty adjusting when his mother's serious illness interfered with his usual routine. The unplanned and changing circumstances tore him away from the safety of his controlled environment and made him feel anxious over how to balance his time.

The word "obsessive" has been used to describe more than a handful of men. We sometimes use it affectionately, in a teasing sense, but we imply that the need to control every detail and every possible outcome is unhealthy. We also suggest in our good-natured humor that excessive control causes us to miss the big picture.

In fact, excessive control keeps us from being bigger and better men. While intending to gain a sense of security through control, we sabotage our spiritual freedom. When we try to control life at all costs, we cannot experience it as it naturally unfolds.

Thomas was one of the first long-term clients I saw as a psychotherapist. Calm and deliberate, Thomas was easy to talk with but difficult to get close to. At age thirty-six, he was still mired in graduate school. He had suffered there for ten years, unable to complete his doctorate in a science-related field. Yet surprisingly, Thomas seemed unaffected and unemotional about his predicament.

Thomas was bright and articulate. Until writing his dissertation, he had controlled his academic circumstances expertly, breezing through his course work. But at the final stages of his education, Thomas was riddled with conflict. The nature of his field required him to allow others to help him with his project; even worse, he would have to allow a dissertation committee to evaluate his work. The prospect of leaving such a crucial decision to others, of placing himself in their hands, was too much for Thomas to deal with. So he protected himself by remaining in graduate school interminably.

"I would like to finish," Thomas acknowledged, "but I don't want to get all upset about it. My wife suggested that I come here for help. To be honest, no offense to you, but I would rather work this out myself."

Five or six months later, Thomas was prepared to let me help him. Once we explored some of the reasons for his conflict—his need to maintain control, his fear of anxiety and fear of experiencing the life of an adult—Thomas began to make steady progress with his dissertation. He was particularly affected by a comment I made one morning. I explained that in his extreme need to control his work and his emotions, he had actually lost some control over his life over the past ten years.

Ultimately Thomas graduated and moved to the West Coast, where he began a job in research, a dream of his that had remained dormant during his struggle. For Thomas, relinquished control gave him renewed self-confidence and faith. Thomas had allowed himself to grow up emotionally and professionally.

Thomas's situation was extreme, but many of us allow our need for control to dominate us for years. By relinquishing this tie, we open ourselves up to a variety of experiences and opportunities. The most important of these is renewed faith, which is really what we are defending against through our efforts at control. It is never too late to learn the importance of letting go. The mystery of faith, with all its hopefulness, awaits. We must be able to say for ourselves: "My heart knows no fear" (Ps. 27:3).

*On the Road Toward Faith*

We are slow to realize that inner peace and emotional experience are requisite for faith. Faith in God is more than an idea or a single feeling. It is an experience, a collection of ideas and feelings, that arises in the individual. As we leap toward God, it is the strange and mysterious phenomenon of faith that makes us whole.

"Do I have a lot of faith?" questioned Wade, a twenty-eight-year-old hotel employee, rhetorically. "I don't know if

I could tell you what faith is. I'm not sure anybody can. I mean, how do you know if what you think you believe is what you really believe? Faith isn't exactly a thing you can carry in your hands."

We do not come by faith easily. Once we have struggled with residual anger and resentment and have left behind our rigid adherence to control, faith is tenable, but there is no convenient method or road map for sustaining it. Most of us have to fight to gain our faith and then remain steadfast to maintain it. It can be a formidable fight indeed, but it is noble for a man to "fight the good fight of faith" (1 Tim. 6:12, KJV).

But more specifically, what is this "faith" that requires so much work before we can entertain its presence in our lives?

Faith may be defined as an ardent belief in something that is not a consensual fact and therefore cannot be proven or disproven. Since faith is not reducible to conventional evidence and proof, it makes men uneasy; we like to be certain and precise about everything we do.

Faith may also be considered from a more philosophical point of view. In *The Meaning and End of Religion,* Wilfred Cantwell Smith offers a compelling distinction: "Theology is part of the traditions of the world. Faith lies beyond theology, in the hearts of men. Truth lies beyond faith, in the heart of God. The very fact that the heart is so central to this perspective implies that the religious experience is highly emotional. That can render us more than a bit tentative, for it compels us to confront an area of considerable avoidance, the inner emotional life."

The Bible itself offers other interpretations of faith. One of the most direct and vivid discussions of faith occurs in Hebrews 1 and continues through several succeeding pas-

THE SOUL OF A MAN

sages. The treatment of faith is so pragmatic and accessible that it sounds like a modern point of view.

"What is faith?" the passage begins. "It is the confident assurance that something we want is going to happen. It is the certainty that what we hope for is waiting for us, even though we cannot see it up ahead. Men of God in days of old were famous for their faith" (Heb. 11:1–2).

"By faith," the passage continues, "by believing God, we know that the world and the stars, in fact, all things, were made at God's command; and that they were all made from things that can't be seen" (Heb. 11:3).

The search for a God who is invisible tests the faith of every man. Not only are we compelled to struggle with faith in everyday matters, but we are forced to ponder what it means to believe in a single, unitary God.

Through our seeking we realize that faith in God requires the highest terms of faith. Why? Because God is by definition invisible and unimaginable. Because faith in a Supreme Being demands total commitment. It is impossible to go halfway when it comes to God. God demands a high form of faith because our relationship with Him is private, highly individualized, and different from any other relationship. This faith transcends life. Faith in God may be nurtured by others, but a man accepts God in the shadows of his aloneness. That apparent solitude makes this form of faith *the most demanding of all*—and the most rewarding.

"When I began to believe in God," stated thirty-three-year-old Philip, a restaurant manager, "I was living in a studio in Los Angeles, away from my family. I was lonely, searching, even a little desperate at times. With each day, I believed a little more; it was a gradual thing. Slowly, good people started coming into my life. I've been changing ever since."

Philip's testament brings us to another key aspect of faith: it can serve as a building block for masculinity. Certainly that theme is relevant to all of us, young men and old men, men of formal religious background and men of informal soul-searching. "One's nationality or race or education or social position is unimportant" (Col. 3:11).

Faith in God is our essential source of masculine development; He is the mortar for our most ambitious undertakings. How? By providing meaning for living. With faith in God, a man's actions are no longer arbitrary and isolated; they are meaningful and significant. As a believer in God, a man can not wallow in anger or excessive control any longer, for the work of God beckons him.

Faith in God also supplies a man with needed structure by giving him reasonable values and guidelines to live by. These spiritual guidelines are not a rigid set of rules, though some of narrow vision may interpret them that way. They reflect a general moral approach to life that we can apply pragmatically to everyday experiences. Through this practical provision of structure, spiritual teaching, and philosophy, a man finds an ally in his efforts to sustain his masculinity.

Faith also enhances masculinity by helping a man determine his own power and limitations. The angry man does not know his own power or powerlessness, but the man of God knows himself well. And he understands his relation to God. He knows that genuine power comes from God, yet he does not fear his stature relative to God. He sees what he can accomplish in the world and how he might serve God in fine fashion. The man of faith also recognizes that he needs other people, just as he needs God.

"Every day I thank God for the kind of family and friends I have," observed Michael, a gregarious telephone executive in his late thirties. "Where would I be now if it weren't for my dad, who taught me about savvy in business? Where would I be without my wife, Ginny, whose love has never wavered and who has raised our kids to respect us even when I haven't been perfect? The world would be a lot duller place if it weren't for the folks I work with; if it weren't for them, there'd be nobody to tease, nobody to complain about the Red Sox to! Thank God for all of them."

Ultimately faith fortifies the masculine soul by creating a spirit of optimism and hope. With God, what reason is there for a man to be disconsolate? Faith in God allows a man a glimpse of a world where all things are possible. A broken relationship can make room for a new and richer opportunity. Fighting the noble fight of faith opens up new vistas, for God enables a man to dream and to hope. And "there is one ray of hope; His compassion never ends" (Lam. 3:21).

*Experiencing Faith in Our Daily Lives*

The best place to look for faith is in our personal experiences. Through the events and conversations in our lives, God weaves His wonderful yet simple magic.

Our openness to faith often surprises us, but it shouldn't. We all have a natural and understandable need for God that is part of our being.

God surprises us, too, by the down-to-earth way He manifests Himself. Occasionally we experience a striking episode or vision of faith; these events, called epiphanies, are breakthroughs for us, in which we see God's presence in the midst of our everyday experiences.

I cannot say that I have dramatic epiphanies every day, but some of the spiritual relationships I have formed represent small epiphanies.

One such relationship is my friendship with Bob, who owns a neighborhood barbershop around the corner from where I live. Bob has operated that barbershop for over twenty years; I'm the one who is new in the neighborhood. The same could be said for the territory of faith and spirituality as well.

Bob is a dark, pleasant-looking man who appears a bit younger than his fifty years. When I entered his old-fashioned barbershop for the first time, it was because I was frustrated and disgruntled with the various trendy and pseudostylish salons in the area. I went in for a decent haircut and proceeded to do so each month. But with every visit, I also left his shop with a good deal of spiritual guidance and even a little more faith.

The barbershop is full of the usual paraphernalia of the trade—brushes, scissors, shaving cream, conditioners, and a distinctive men's barbershop smell. But there is something different about Bob's place. Amid the tools of the haircutting business, a number of religious items decorate and enrich the small shop. Bob is a devout Catholic, and God is the central figure in his life. For Bob, there is no artificial separation of work and personal life. He brings the Lord with him to work through his manner and his philosophy of life. Bob believes in God with all his soul.

Bob does not impose his religious views on his clientele. But anyone interested in spiritual matters may be treated to a frank and honest talk about Bob's own history and views.

When I first talked to Bob about spirituality, my anger and need to control situations got in the way. I could not truly listen to what he was saying. I don't need another lecture about God, I thought defensively.

Gradually my uneasiness subsided. I began to listen more intently to Bob and to share more of my own views. Bob helped me express my ideas about God, faith, and doubt. He helped me through my longstanding spiritual diffidence and helped me realize that "my heart had great experience of wisdom" (Eccles. 1:16, KJV).

The lessons Bob taught me about faith are extensive, real-world notions about a man's personal journey. It is difficult to summarize them, but most revolve around the strength of faith necessary for personal fulfillment.

"Life is full of ideas and beliefs," Bob might say, "but a man has to decide what *he* really believes. You can depend on other people for a lot of things, but sometimes, because they are human, they may disappoint you. Only God won't disappoint, as He speaks through the silence of a man's heart. God has a great record of reliability, but you have to have faith in Him."

In everyone's life, people like Bob are ready to offer sound spiritual advice and guidance. We just have to be open to them. Bob and good men like him are keepers of faith, messengers who help others by relating to their own experiences and by caring about us as men.

I am thankful to have Bob as a friend and also grateful that there are others like Bob in the world. Bob's presence reminds me that no man needs to be alone in the world, for the spirit of God will journey with him. It is all a matter of faith.

One of the religious items hanging on the wall in Bob's barbershop is the insightful religious vignette "Footprints," which is a testament to the human journey and God's role in our own lives. Like Bob's spiritual insights, it speaks of the essence of a man's faith:

## FOOTPRINTS

One night a man had a dream. He dreamed he was walking along the beach with the Lord. Across the sky flashed scenes from his life. For each scene, he noticed two sets of footprints in the sand; one belonging to him and the other to the Lord. When the last scene of his life flashed before him, he looked back at the footprints in the sand. He noticed that many times along the path of his life there was only one set of footprints. He also noticed that it happened at the very lowest and saddest times in his life. This really bothered him and he questioned the Lord about it. "Lord, you said that once I decided to follow you, you'd walk with me all the way. But I have noticed that during the most troublesome times in my life, there is only one set of footprints. I don't understand why when I needed you most you would leave me." The Lord replied, "My precious, precious child, I love you and I would never leave you. During your times of trial and suffering, when you see only one set of footprints, it was then that I carried you." (Anonymous)

# PART 2

# EXPRESSIONS OF THE SOUL

# CHAPTER 6

# THE MALE
# WORK ETHIC

**B**usiness is picking up," quipped Joey, age thirty-eight
and the owner of a small bakery. "Picking up whatever garbage you've left around so you can go home! Let's face it,
you live for working. It's a grind. But you spend more time
working than anything else. It's just the way it is. You can
lie to yourself, but work dominates a person's life. And it
determines how other guys see you. Your work is who you
are."

Men are often equated with the work they do, as if we
could determine a man's worth to society by his work alone.
Performance is the irrefutable yardstick we accept as a standard long before we know anything about salaries or stocks.
We learn about performance in our first Little League game
or at our first grade school science fair, if not sooner. The
girls who sat next to us in grade school had to perform as

well, but not to the same extent. Achievement was and still is more crucial for men.

Is this emphasis on achievement and competitiveness good for us? Under what circumstances does it make us better men, and under what conditions does it erode our sense of worth? Once instilled in the five-year-old or the ten-year-old, is this preoccupation with performance irreversible, or are we capable of mastering a better means to evaluate ourselves?

Some critical questions emerge when we consider our work lives. To what degree do the initiatives we assume in the world bring us closer to fulfillment or take us further away from it? For better or worse, performance is a social phenomenon that all men must grapple with. Some will seek success through sweat and struggle; others will seek truth through reflection and resolve. Whatever our pathway, "there is a time there for every purpose and for every [form of] work" (Eccles. 3:17, KJV).

*How I Learned About Achievement*

In addition to the mundane work and life challenges that we encounter, most of us attempt to find "a big project" or "a big event" with which to test ourselves. The project or event can be a job, a competitive confrontation, an intellectual enigma to be solved, or a block of granite to be moved— it makes no difference. What matters is that we perceive the task to be a major hurdle.

My first attempt to tackle the big project occurred during college. To graduate from Harvard with honors in a specific field, students had to complete an original thesis. Consideration for highest honors, or summa cum laude, required a thesis that made some new and profound contribution. My classmates and I understood that much would be required of us if we wished to pursue that lofty goal.

I set my academic course toward that formidable challenge. Was it the need for self-respect that motivated me? I am still not certain. I decided to do a research study and an accompanying thesis, bigger and better than anything I had done before. My choice of a topic, "Children of Concentration Camp Survivors," was readily understandable given my background. The person I sought out as an adviser was no less interesting. If you want to go all out and try for all the academic accolades, I reasoned, you may as well find someone who knows all about academic success. Through persistence and a bit of good fortune, I procured the guidance of Professor David C. McClelland, the man who coined the concept of "achievement motivation" and has written extensively about achievement and power. That fact made my choice of him as adviser no simple coincidence.

Professor McClelland looked like Buffalo Bill. He even had a picture of the western hero on his door. It was the first thing I noticed and the last thing I remembered about Professor McClelland. Behind the good-natured humor was a great deal of seriousness and drive.

McClelland's work on motives—and the achievement motive in particular—had spanned three decades and a number of teaching appointments. Through the 1970s, his work expanded to include significant contributions on power motivation, alcoholism, and cross-cultural differences. Unlike many other psychologists, he wrote simply and clearly, and his ideas had the mark of a brilliant generalist. His views touched upon politics, religion, and anthropology as often as psychology. Yet, during my undergraduate years, the concept of achievement motivation fascinated me more than anything.

"It's not just a matter of working hard," McClelland would sometimes startle me by saying, "because if it were, we'd be looking at performance, not the desire to achieve. Achievement motivation is more than that, and it works more efficiently than that for most people. To be moved to achieve is to pursue a standard of excellence with great vigor. And there's another interesting point about it," he would add. "It's not competing against other people—that's an American business misnomer—it's testing yourself against a measure of high excellence."

When McClelland spoke, I always wrote down as much as I could, as if it would vanish if I relegated it to memory alone. The confidence with which he spoke captivated me. I enjoyed his expansive ideas and appreciated how they often inspired curiosity in me. In him I saw a healthy merger of work and play—a blend guided more by his own interests than by outside demands or considerations. He seemed to live by the maxim "I . . . applied my heart unto every work" (Eccles. 8:9, KJV).

"The seeds of achievement motivation can be found in the early mother-child relationship, especially for boys," McClelland would say with great certainty. "Mothers who are very involved with their children, even making plentiful demands and restrictions, are more likely to produce motivated youngsters. It's particularly true if cultural values and ideology, as with the Japanese, encourage achievement."

The connection between achievement and childhood intrigued me. It brought me back to my early grade school days, my patterns of work and play, and my own achievement training. For many people something must go awry; how else could so many of us work obsessively, rather than constructively, and allow such compulsive work to dominate our lives?

McClelland taught me about working hard, but he also showed me that industry makes sense only when it is connected to values and faith. His travels to third world countries and his interest in understanding political problems from a psychological angle supported that idea. But the respectful, encouraging way he treated me, the inexperienced but eager undergraduate, also said a great deal about the way he embraced his work. Our task was to work together on an intellectual project, but he also helped me to bring humaneness to whatever I did. For without a sense of values and humanity, no achievement, no work outcome, and no performance criterion has enduring worth.

When I graduated with highest honors, I knew that I owed David McClelland a debt of gratitude. If college is supposed to teach a person how to think, not what to think, then I was most fortunate indeed. I had also learned something about how to live. My work relationship with Professor McClelland deepened my faith in other people and helped me to focus on what is important in a man's work—its relationship to spiritual and psychological matters. Later I would come to realize that "my work [was] with my God" (Isa. 49:4, KJV).

*Dealing with the Reality of Making a Living*

My undergraduate lessons were challenged several years later when it was time to earn a living. Ideals concerning achievement, however noble, meet their stiffest opposition in the pragmatics of financial survival. Indeed, as I entered the adult world, it became clear to me that maintaining a focus on pure achievement was not going to be easy.

For me, as for most men, a series of built-in obstacles made meaningful achievement more difficult than mere financial success. I often wonder: How is it possible for a man to achieve in the way that he wants to achieve?

As with most things that have affected me so personally, I have formed a few generalized impressions about what young men and women run into these days in the development of a career. I had to overcome a series of successive roadblocks in order to be myself. Many other men must face similar roadblocks.

From my experiences in psychology, academia, and the publishing world, and from my conversations with friends in law, medicine, business, and other diverse fields, I have concluded that most young men specialize too early and are then almost forced by circumstances to adhere to that specialty. The fledgling lawyer is urged to choose tax law, for example, while the doctor in training is compelled to decide on pediatrics or surgery.

But specialization presents problems. First, a man who commits to a specialty early in life cannot explore a variety of career possibilities, and that may be a significant factor in midlife crisis. How can an individual who is still in the process of becoming an adult choose his lifelong work when his values will almost definitely change with maturity? Most of us have to make career decisions shortly after graduation, and that places us in a poor position to choose an occupation that matches our deepest personal interests and aspirations. Before we realize what is happening, the work treadmill speeds up, making it tricky for us to get off and indeed unlikely that we will do so. This leaves us disappointed with our jobs and unfulfilled in our creative potential.

Second, fewer and fewer jobs are ideological or philosophical in nature. Computers are a wonderful and time-saving human advancement, but with them have come a proliferation of neutral, passionless, and limited jobs. Too many modern jobs do not cultivate higher values.

Roger, age thirty-three, discussed his dilemma. "I went to a very good liberal arts school. You start out being curious about a lot of things, and then something happens. Snap. All of a sudden you're working at the same thing for seven years. I'm a systems analyst, and I make about forty-five thousand a year. But do I care about what I do? Not all that much. I'm resigned that work is work."

The less ideological a job is, the less likely it is to fit a man's perspective on life. The job may not offend that perspective or threaten it, but it will not present the opportunity for fuller achievement either. If a man does not feel passionate about his occupation, he may do an adequate job, but he will not cultivate meaning.

The paucity of jobs related to psychology, religion, and life perspective directly influences our career choices. If these subjects are not part and parcel of our work lives, then it is likely we will spend less time engaged with them. That will mean less time devoted to our inner motives, the source of achievement. Ironically, we are dangerously close to cutting ourselves off from the inspiration for true achievement.

Third, jobs that demand more and more evening time force us to choose work over family life and extracurricular concerns. A reduction of free time can mean a reduction in the opportunity for free thought, or at least less of a chance for reflection about how our lives are going and how our jobs fit into the greater scheme of things. As "nine to five" has increasingly become a thing of the past for so many, a sense of detachment from the self is almost unavoidable. But to keep from being automatons, we must realize it is best to do "the work of this house of God" (Ezra 6:7, KJV).

These developments accentuate the stress on performance and thus increase stress—the inevitable fallout from excess pressure. We forget our individual needs as a consequence of work demands. Most of our jobs, whether white collar or blue collar, do little to inspire our thinking about ethics, community, and society at large. We exist as a small part of a vast sociological puzzle, unable to see the larger puzzle. As individuals, we lose sight of our internal standards and our propensities for meaningful achievement.

Milton, a fifty-one-year-old executive, reflected on his career. "When I started out, I was really all-company. I was very gung ho. But as time goes on, you realize you have to look out for yourself in the company. Most of business does not respect the individual. You have to protect your self-respect. You have to always keep your family and yourself in mind."

## The Male Work Ethic

Given that these pressures impinge upon most men, how do we respond?

It's my conviction that many men react with a stance I call the "Male Work Ethic." It's a common response, which, while possessing some clear virtues, also has severe liabilities. It's our way of coping with the demands of breadwinning and the modern emphasis on performance at any cost.

The Male Work Ethic has several principles, each of

which takes shape in discernible ways. First, it suggests that hard work will reap its own benefits. If we adopt that philosophy, as many of us seem to do, we will blindly persevere even when the purpose of our work is unclear or nonexistent. Applying the principle can be an act of faith, but often it carries with it a less constructive, compulsive quality. When that happens, our pursuit of the dollar can be very self-defeating, and money becomes a "defense" (Eccles. 7:12, KJV).

Consider the point of view of Curt, a thirty-nine-year-old writer. "Why do I keep writing? I've asked myself that many times. It certainly isn't for money or fame, because I've had very little of that. I don't really love it either. I think you'd have to be crazy to love writing. I guess I think that working hard pays off. I suppose I'm conservative in that way. It's what I learned from my father, and I keep believing it's true. So what if the payoff takes a long time?"

A second principle of the Male Work Ethic is that men define themselves by the kind of work they do. Male lawyers are inclined to see themselves as argumentative and shrewd, while male professors tend to view themselves as cerebral and, depending upon their fields, either scientific or poetic. I don't believe that women define themselves as much by their professions. Women seem to keep in greater touch with their emotional sides, and their views of themselves tend to reflect that accordingly.

Third, the Male Work Ethic encourages men to see work as a way of life. Living is synonymous with making a living, not with leisure or reflection. It is habitually important for most men to keep active; work is the most active thing they do. To step back from work, except for highly scheduled and structured vacations, is considered passive and irresponsible.

It threatens the order of things, at least from the male perspective. Many men would be exceedingly nervous about living the life-style of their housewife spouses, yet they sometimes envy their wives' apparent freedom and lack of structure. It is hard for us to relate to an absence of structure, since we have not acknowledged our own need for it.

"I don't know how my wife does it," blurted out forty-five-year-old Alex, a mass transit employee. "I'd go nuts not working. I wouldn't know what to do with the day. I wouldn't get anything done around the house. Especially now that the kids are in their teens. I don't know how she keeps from getting bored day in and day out."

Alex and those of us who reflect this ethic reveal a fourth quality. We have learned not to question the work we do because we believe it cannot be changed or improved—even if our status or position could grant us greater creative freedom. We lack faith in the process of change. Owing to a debilitating, underlying cynicism, we see work as predestined and unalterable. We see our daily routine as inevitable. That way of thinking reflects a fundamental pessimism, which we transfer onto the work world and sometimes to life in general. We sense our own rigidity and believe that the circumstances of our lives are fixed. That simply is not true. All change is possible with God and with a man's faith.

Fifth, we too readily accept a distinct separation of work and leisure. We tend to compartmentalize our lives into "work time" and "leisure time," delegating certain activities and moods to each. I have come to believe, however, that the men who are most fulfilled do not forge such a definite division. They go about their vacations with a spirit of leisure and inner calm. On the other hand, their work is typified by a richness and a zealousness. They have mastered the art of working effortlessly and playing vigorously, and their lives show few of the strains of a segmented existence. The balance is difficult to achieve, but it carries considerable rewards. A man needs to be undivided in the pursuits of his life.

Since most of us do not achieve so effortlessly, what are the personal ramifications of the Male Work Ethic for us? Many men have difficulty feeling content and meeting their needs for achievement. I have also observed trouble with relational and interpersonal needs when work psychology is awry. I am certain that the inclination to be controlled by our jobs makes it hard for us to let go of work, even at retirement. In fact, the Male Work Ethic may not even foster efficiency, for it doesn't really include an internalized standard of excellence. By its nature, the Male Work Ethic leaves us feeling less than potent and prevents us from seeking higher ideals, such as the kind of personal peace that is again "better . . . than fine gold" (Prov. 3:14, KJV).

The work picture is not quite that bleak. Some men are reasonably content with their jobs. But our drive for achievement is innate and will surface and resurface as a response to meaningless sweat and thoughtless compulsion. Ultimately our psychological and spiritual needs for efficacy and important work will have to be met. In our lives "the works of God should be made manifest" (John 9:3, KJV). But we must find fresh and creative ways to pursue enduring achievement.

*My Efforts at Personal Achievement*

So what is to be done about work? Because I've followed an unconventional career path, I've had the opportunity to do a lot of soul-searching about work and achievement. I've tried very hard, at the expense of money and comfort, to come up with an occupational pathway that makes sense to me. The key is to find something that suits a person's individuality. This is a task much easier outlined than accomplished. But a certain tolerance for uncertainty and an ability to delay immediate reward do offer reason for hope. Faith does not hurt, either. "Since we are His children, we will share His treasure" (Rom. 8:16).

Contrary to what I would have expected, being an author has not in itself resolved the question of work for me. Writing does seem to offer freedom of expression and an opportunity for satisfying achievement. The nature of writing, with its solitude and reflection, would seem to call upon deeply felt standards of excellence. But writing, like most other fields, demands an homage to absurd grit and trivia—an homage that I am not willing to pay as a matter of course.

No, my resolution is not a single means of expression alone. I'm not sure that can ever work for any man. The psyche is too complex and the soul too rich for that, despite our inner doubts and protests to the contrary.

What has worked for me, or more accurately, what is in an evolutionary process of working for me, is focusing on what I have to say rather than on the form it takes. That means concentrating on ideas or inner values rather than the process of work, whether it's verbal, physical, written, or otherwise. I have found that concentrating on the essence of experience helps me reach for my best and takes me deeper into my soul. For example, it helps me to concentrate on the content of what I have to say, whether it's about men, children, or families, rather than how many books are sold or how the publishing world measures success. Such a posture also seems to bring me closer to God. "All his works are done in truth" (Ps. 33:4, KJV).

The vocational changes a man makes need not be drastic, nor do they necessitate a move from one field to another. But I do believe that a man must be attentive to his inner changes and try to adjust his work life accordingly. In these decisions, "the Lord will be our light" (Isa. 60:20).

Achievement is most significant when it comes from the deepest motivations of an individual, not from externally imposed motives and interests. So I move across topics and keep open to what form my inner life will take. The knowledge that another change may be overshadowed by the sensation that I am growing closer to my soul matters to me a great deal. I believe it should matter to all men. The greatest achievement of all is the development of the soul, where performance and perspiration are background concerns. Soulwork is a lifetime vocation, and we need to be solidly employed and fully engaged. The soul is its own standard of excellence, and it works at a special kind of work—God's work. We can take pride in our involvement in that work, for "the works of the Lord are great" (Ps. 111:2, KJV).

# CHAPTER 7

# THE GAMES MEN PLAY

**W**hen Mookie Wilson hit that ground ball through Buckner's legs in the sixth game of the '86 Series, time just stood still," commented Ray, age forty-one. "I've been a Red Sox fan all my life, and that moment kind of sums it up. But still I watch them win or lose. I guess it gets into your blood, or else we're all crazy!"

When you live in Boston, as I do, Boston Garden and Fenway Park are as much a part of revered tradition as the Old North Church and the Bunker Hill Monument. These athletic shrines are as popular as any historical attraction. What inspires us to worship at these sports arenas so fervently through our steadfast attendence? What makes men so fascinated by sports?

An interest in sports starts early for most of us. Our fledgling experiences of "pitcher and catcher" probably occurred well before we could read. Little League fields represented an initial test of the inner spirit. When it came to matters of the heart, each Little League game was like a pennant clincher. Each victory or defeat was acted out in front of a huge audience of fifty, which typically included our parents.

Soon we also developed a spectator's enthusiasm for professional sports and became addicted. Professional sports provide us a wonderful opportunity for release. In fact, they're our special form of leisure and gamesmanship. Jim Lampley, former ABC sports commentator and currently with HBO, summed it up well when he said: "If you grow up in America, you have to be affected by men in sports. Even if you aren't involved in athletics, sports reflects society's values in the microcosm of play."

### The View from the Broadcast Booth

I sought out Jim Lampley concerning his views about men and athletics in America for two reasons. First, among members of his generation of sportscasters, his resumé seemed the most varied and comprehensive. Among other major events, Lampley has covered the summer and winter Olympics, the Super Bowl, the Indianapolis 500, the Kentucky Derby, college football, numerous major boxing matches, including Douglas *vs.* Tyson, and many golf matches. That seemed like quite a range of events to me, a vantage point that would allow Lampley accurately to generalize about the purpose of sports in our lives. Second, his analysis of these events was articulate and unusually reflective. He seemed to have an appreciation for the psychological and spiritual dimensions of sport that transcended the final scores and results.

The ABC sports department, renowned for its Olympics coverage, "Wide World of Sports," and the fact that Howard Cosell matriculated there, occupies several floors. When I arrived, Lampley was seated at his desk, negotiating between some publicity material about Patrick Ewing and a phone call about a golf tournament he was to cover. After we exchanged comments about Gary Carter's three home runs the night before, our talk about sports and masculinity began.

Jim Lampley was able to sum up the pluses and minuses of sports with considerable balance and insight. He suspended his own sarcasm about the more materialistic side of professional athletics, and focused on what sports offer to men. He acknowledged that the contributions of sports are nebulous, such as improving our lives through leisure and dissolving tensions. But then Lampley spoke about his own childhood, the loss of his father at a young age, and the importance of sports in his own life. Sometimes, because of a loss in his life, a person must "climb up some other way" (John 10:2).

"As the world is becoming increasingly complex and confused," Lampley said with more feeling than when he spoke about sports heroes and statistics, "sports is a way you can anchor yourself . . . with simple precepts and images. You can find your way on the sports pages."

Finding our way—that's one thing that sports seems to do for us. It gives us a sense of structure and purpose, which, if not taken to excess, can provide a healthy outlet throughout childhood and beyond. The images of sport—the record-breaking Aaron home run or the Payton touchdown—offer us pleasant memories and dreams to think about and aspire toward. "Play skillfully with a loud noise" (Ps. 33:3)—it's written in relation to music, but it applies to athletics as well.

But, as Lampley was quick to point out, that's only half the picture. Professional athletics and high-profile, high-revenue college sports present a darker side as well. A number of things about contemporary sports tarnish the true nature of what men strive to be. According to Lampley, sports sometimes presents questionable role modeling and values to young men. Sometimes we excuse maniacal behavior in the heat of an athletic contest that would be reprehensible on a city street or in the schoolyard. We stretch the definition of manly behavior to include aggressive behavior in the pursuit of victory. There are any number of illustrations of this in football, baseball, basketball, hockey, and other popular sports. Lampley cited the example of highly volatile and controversial Indiana basketball coach Bobby Knight.

"Society places such a high value on winning, and Bobby Knight has benefited greatly from this," Lampley asserted. "Winning," he continued philosophically, "in the public eye, overshadows other deficiencies of character. Despite [Bobby Knight's] obvious imbalances, a great deal has been excused."

A second dilemma for men, implicit in Lampley's other comments, is a prevalent hypocrisy and inflated sense of importance about major sports and about media coverage of these events. Professional sports too often rely upon fanfare and media hype, rather than allowing the substance of the games to speak for themselves. "Honor the Lord with your substance" (Prov. 3:9). The result for men and for boys is considerable phoniness and misrepresentation of the games they love. Instead of emphasizing the soulfulness of the sports experience, television concentrates on commercialization and glitter.

Lampley noted his personal experience with the Super Bowl as a case in point. "The Super Bowl is easily the most overblown and overpromoted event in American society," he bluntly stated. "The attention it receives is hard to believe. And that comes from a guy who has done the game and its two-hour pregame show!"

If you add the subject of violence to Lampley's concerns about the negative effects of sport, you have a good summary of the major issues that should concern us as men. When I left his office that day, I felt as if I had received a good overview of the double-edged nature of sports and sportsmen today. I had seen one sportscaster's ambivalence firsthand, a striking glimpse of his zeal as well as his disappointments about the focus of his passion, the sports world.

Like so many men, Jim Lampley seemed fascinated by the world of sports and had made it an integral part of his life. Lampley seemed privy to the incredibly mixed messages that the contemporary sports world sends to men. These messages are an integral part of spectator sports in particular, but they also find their way to the weekend warriors who traverse our amateur playing fields and greens.

### How Do Sports Affect Men?

Since my meeting with Jim Lampley, my understanding about the role of sports in our lives has grown. It's not that I enjoy sports less, but I see their importance and sometimes exaggerated role a bit more vividly.

Time and time again, I hear men talk about the team concept inherent in many of our most popular games. Though the team concept is threatened by today's exorbitant salaries, free agency, and arbitration, it remains an excellent

way to teach boys and young men how to get along with one
another for a greater goal. We are to live in harmony with
our brothers (Matt. 5:24). Perhaps because of their greater
socialization in sports, boys tend to learn about the team
concept earlier and more convincingly than do girls.

Certain sports figures have become famous for their dedication to the team concept, including such legends as Vince
Lombardi and Red Auerbach. Bo Schembechler, the recently
retired coach of the University of Michigan, is known as an
unparalleled communicator of the team concept. Although
Michigan teams have frequently been applauded because of
the stalwart cohesiveness of their defensive units, Schembechler remained their demanding professor. He lectured
about his theory of the team concept: "No player is more
important than the team—The Team! The Team! The
Team!" How many among us learned that in one form or
another as children? How many of us yearn for that kind of
camaraderie today?

In addition to the team ideal, sports provide men with an
opportunity to confront and learn about their limitations.
These limitations may be mental and emotional, but in nearly
all athletic challenges, a physical limitation must be tackled.
Athletics can teach us about struggling in the face of adver-
sity and running "with patience" (Heb. 12:1). It can also
show us when that is unwise.

Often, the prime example of struggling with a limitation
is having a sports injury. Most of us admire a prominent
athlete who plays with pain, risking further injury. But sometimes we wonder if he might be foolish, even a bit crazy.
Playing with pain is part of the male sports bravado, but it
can also represent a soulful act of dedication and discipline.

Most of us have memories of great moments in sport. In

some of those, the struggle with limitations, not the eventual outcome, mattered most. One of my favorite moments occurred in the 1984 summer Olympics.

Bert Cameron, a Jamaican middle-distance runner, was a favorite in the four-hundred-meter race. During the semifinals, Cameron suddenly pulled up lame in this fast-paced race. Any hope of reaching the finals seemed instantly lost. Then, shockingly, out of the midst of his agony, Cameron kept running—so well, in fact, that he miraculously completed the race and made the finals. Shortly thereafter, a sports correspondent named Bud Greenspan wrote of this extraordinary accomplishment:

"Bert Cameron showed incredible courage when he cramped in his hamstring and pulled up short as the rest of the field passed him. He then suddenly took off again, some 40 meters behind, made up the distance and qualified for the final. It did not matter that his torn hamstring kept him out of the final. He had competed with honor."

Such images of dignity and perseverance touch all of us. They stay with us long after the last event has been run and the last symbolic flame has been extinguished. Sports can provide us an opportunity to find meaning in the process of competing. Sports embody the perseverance of the human spirit, and this steadfast demeanor can bring enjoyment, which "is the gift of God" (Eccles. 3:13).

Along with teaching and demonstrating, sports are just plain fun. They allow men, and women too, to feel excited in ways we might otherwise think childish or overemotional. Sports allow us to "let go" and provide us with excitement that we may have difficulty finding elsewhere. The exhilaration of physical expression is not inhibited in sports. Whether it's the "Michael Jordan Slam" or the "Icky Shuffle," sports allow us to express ourselves without inhibition.

Excitement is a central characteristic of all sports, and for men in all sports. It comes in all shapes and sizes, from seven-foot basketball players to five-foot jockeys. If men need emotion to be complete, then sports certainly offer a ready-made, if sometimes contrived, opportunity to acquire it. While most occupations inhibit and contain passion, sports embody it. Sports events are dramatic events. And, according to National Basketball Association representative Brian McIntyre, whom I spoke with by phone, "the real key to the popularity of sport is that the drama is live."

John, a twenty-seven-year-old sports enthusiast, expressed a similar sentiment. "I love sports because there is so much action. Like in hockey, it's end to end. Scores are usually unpredictable—unless somebody like Wayne Gretzsky is playing. Going to a game, especially hockey or basketball, where you can sit closer to the action, makes me feel more energized. That's a good feeling."

Luis, age thirty, added: "The Bo Jackson thing shows what sports is about. His playing two sports is fantastic, not just 'cause he gets paid a million dollars for a hobby, but because he plays the best. He's awesome. People come to the game just to watch Bo play. I saw a clip on TV where they showed thousands of people came to the ballpark early just to watch him take batting practice!"

But against the buildup of camaraderie, challenge, and excitement, sports present some disturbing contributions to our understanding of how men behave.

Excessive violence is a way of life in a number of sports. As in the hockey brawl or the baseball beanballing, athletics provide opportunities for aggression rather than a spectrum of artistic and creative possibilities. For example, former Miami Dolphin wide receiver Nat Moore captured the pervading atmosphere in football when he said, "We're the modern gladiators. We're down there for the fans to shout: 'Kill! Kill! Kill!' "

Sports violence has been the focus of several research studies. One study concerned with spectator participation showed that three-quarters of the violent incidents in hockey stands were preceded by fighting on the ice. In a more startling finding, a study in *American Health Magazine* reported that the national homicide rate rose 12.5 percent on the day following a heavyweight championship fight. These and other studies suggest that sports, despite their merits, can become a rationale and a symbol for misguided passion.

Sports can inspire masculine dreams and passions, but they can also bring out less socialized and constructive motives. To the extent that sports sanction violence, then they turn us away from a balanced and sensible attitude about leisure. They also lead us away from a soulful life-style that partakes of leisure.

A second harmful aspect of many sports is the emphasis on winning over sportsmanship. Sometimes it seems that sportsmanship is at best the background scenery on which competitive pursuit takes place. Winning counts above all else in most sports. Winning and box scores are certainly the obsessive concerns of those who report sports. National Basketball Association representative Brian McIntyre captured the prevailing media orientation when he said to me: "I've yet to read a news story where they don't give the score and say instead that the athletes played like gentlemen."

With an individual athlete's worth so often measured by

performance and victory, and not by character, a man is treated as a commodity. But this measurement isn't peculiar to sports. Excessive interest in outcomes and performances is characteristic of men in many other fields, too, especially in business and commerce. To the extent that sports exacerbate this tendency, it reflects a failure to show sufficient respect for inner life and inner values.

"You can get too caught up in wins and losses as a fan," said forty-year-old Ernie. "You forget sometimes that they're human and the purpose is for relaxing. But let's face it. It's not a gentleman's game anymore—even baseball—it's a business, too."

Finally, there is a certain exclusivity that surrounds many sports that discriminates against women. For some of us, sports represent a last bastion of male domination. We protect that bastion with great rigidity and resolve. At the college level, this means less emphasis on women's sports. But at the level of childhood, this may mean few organized athletic activities for girls. What is most rare, with the exception of mixed doubles tennis, is the joint participation and equal involvement of the sexes. Rather than having sports as an exclusive domain, wouldn't it be better for us to "exercise loving kindness" (Jer. 9:24) when it comes to equal participation?

To investigate this theme, I contacted Robin Herman, the former *New York Times* reporter who was the first woman journalist to enter a professional locker room. Herman ventured into the exclusive confines at a National Hockey League all-star game in the Montreal Forum in 1973. She described to me with great intensity the uncomfortable feelings of a woman in the locker room that night, an atmosphere that she feels still exists in sports today. Robin Herman spoke of male sports figures who consider sports a reflection of masculinity alone. These men see women as antithetical to the nature of team sports.

"I remember walking toward the locker room," Herman explained to me. "The guard who might have blocked me out didn't. There were players sitting near their benches. Then suddenly there was a commotion. Players were scattering everywhere, some running to the showers. I tried to talk with Dennis Potvin, but then one of his teammates pulled Potvin's towel away from him!"

The intermingling of the sexes was far from smooth that night in Montreal, just as it has been for sports in general over the years. It is still difficult for men, and perhaps for women also, to see beyond gender in sports. By and large, athletics are often a kind of "jockdom" for which the rights of passage dictate that a man must be rugged and decidedly male. In concluding her recollection, Robin Herman shared her views about gender in sports.

"Most of the men were embarrassed, prudish, even prurient," Herman further explained. "There was a lot of immaturity around sports and its coverage, and I'm not sure that much has changed since."

*Nevertheless, Take Us Out to the Ball Game*

"I don't know what I would do if there was no sports," muses forty-one-year-old Tito. "Watching football on the weekend is how I relax. Even if it's watching the Patriots have no offense because they refuse to play Flutie, it still is worth it. It takes your mind off things and it gives you an excuse to holler your lungs out."

Because of the benefits of athletics, and despite their

problems, most of us embrace sport with great enthusiasm. We may not know how it affects our souls, but we should. Sport is too central in our lives not to affect us in profound ways.

We crave sports as both spectators and participants. Sports offer us a playing field for the spirit, a means by which we can bring together diverse elements of our personalities. Sports allow us to use brawn and brains in a skillful if not playful manner. Sports are our great hobby—the means by which we refresh ourselves and gain a fresh perspective on life. They represent exercise and leisure and an expression of living that is hard for us to find in other pursuits.

These contributions lead to the essence of what makes sports so pleasurable for men. Whether it's basketball or boccie, athletics provide fundamental physical expression. Sports allow us to be highly physical within the clear rules and structure of a game. They help us appreciate the physical tools that God has provided.

"There's just a good feeling about a game of full-court basketball," said twenty-four-year-old Kevin. "Even if it's a pickup game. I don't know if it's the banging bodies, race-horse style, or what, but you lose yourself for a while in the game. And it's kind of like hypnotism. You feel tired afterward, but in a strange way, your body feels really good. Free of tension and cares. It's a kind of high."

Sports give us a psychological lift because they are such a natural vehicle for physical expression. Yet when sport is our sole means of physical expression or when it is separated from other qualities, it fails us terribly. Far from aiding in self-development, it becomes a physical obsession and an unhealthy escape. A man who cannot stop exercising uses sports as a drug. He is a slave to his obsession. But where is his spiritual fitness? By the same token, the professional athlete will live a very limited life after his brief career if he is a one-dimensional person. If sports are to make a significant contribution to our lives, they must open us to the broadest range of experiences and bring mind and body into greater harmony. They must also teach us respect for others and capacity to "honor all men" (1 Pet. 2:17, KJV).

From my discussions with people in professional sports, as well as my talks with other men and my own lifelong love for sports, I know sports has a soulful side. It can contribute significantly to the development of a man's soul. However, sports cannot be a surrogate for the soul, as it seems to be for some of us. When it becomes a preoccupation and not a leisurely avocation, when we are too concerned with our finishing times and not with the run itself, we are running decidedly away from ourselves. We must "rejoiceth as a strong man to run a race" (Ps. 19:5, KJV), not as someone who runs out of fear or obsession.

When sports abandon the dreams and ideals of a man's youth, the athlete may find himself detached from deeper purpose and alienated from his own good sense of leisure.

But it is never too late to stop an unhealthy approach: "The last error is worse than the first" (Matt. 27:64). We must gather ourselves and place sports in a proper perspective. When sports enrich us with an arena for mature physical competition and exchange and the opportunity for equal participation and camaraderie, they further us as individuals and as men. Specifically for men, sports clarify who we are and shape us into who we strive to be. In their best and purest forms, sports can represent health and enjoyment and a fine form of leisure and pleasure.

It is also wise to remember that we owe our physical and spiritual abilities to God, who formed us and has allowed us to strive for athletic accomplishment. In victory as well as defeat, we need God and we need to remember Him:

"They do not conquer by their own strength and skill, but by your mighty power and because you smiled upon them and favored them" (Ps. 44:3).

# CHAPTER 8

# THE SPIRITUALITY OF SEX

I waited in a crowded, poorly lit room with a mixed collection of smiling babies, loud teenagers, and a few other adults. I sat for an hour or so wondering why I was there, whether I fit in, and whether I wanted to fit in. Then a tough-talking young woman screeched out the last name of the fifteen-year-old sitting next to me. I shuddered with a mixture of anger and anxiety. "What am I doing in a modeling agency, anyway?" I asked myself. I sat there for the next few minutes perspiring nervously and trying to hide the sweat. I peered around the room at the Noah's Ark of candidates, unable to focus on myself. It was as if I were waiting for some primordial judgment.

I heard my name called with more callousness than I'd ever heard it pronounced before. The woman with the gravel-filled voice led me unceremoniously to her office, a small room filled with a thousand framed photographs, each indistinguishable except for the peculiar mixture of sexuality and youthfulness on each model's face. Once again I scanned the room looking for understanding and found none. I quickly realized that nothing I had to say mattered at all. Only my appearance mattered. The interviewer was a contest judge, and I was the next contestant. She examined my legs, torso, shoulders, and posture, and stared into my eyes as if they were made of glass and not ideas or feelings. She even called in another judge for a confirming opinion. Calling upon her weak acting skills, the second judge pretended to be looking for a portfolio. It was obvious she was there to check me out, to see if I had the right stuff.

"We're interested in you," the first woman bellowed after the second nodded her approval. The words of acceptance echoed in my ear and mattered to me more than I cared to admit. "Do you realize what you're getting into?" she asked as part of her screening procedure. I had only a dim idea of what she was talking about; the sense of acceptance was still reverberating. Just as I was about to react with a question, any question, the woman with the rough voice responded to her own curiosity: "With all that time you've spent in school, you must know what you're doing." I sat across the way feigning confidence; I had already learned the secret of a plastic smile. I knew in my heart that the woman was wrong. I had no idea what I was doing in a modeling agency, and my soul was somewhere lost and distant.

Having completed graduate school not long before, I was seeking to develop myself in a different way. I had tired of a world where everything was intellectual, and I was searching for something radically different. At the urging of some friends, I tried to push myself into a world that embodied the business of sexuality. I turned toward ephemeral and "vain things" (1 Sam. 12:21, KJV).

My tenure in modeling was both painful and short-lived. I discovered a life-style that lacked substance and respect for individuality. I met many people who had not made peace with themselves nor with their own sense of narcissism. They were still looking for approval in a neon way. Between runway turns and tailoring, I met a fellow who had played a minor role in "Dynasty," agency directors, fashion magazine editors, fashion consultants, and people in advertising and fashion. Whatever their status, I sensed something dehumanizing about their business. The life-style seemed to be particularly harsh for men, who were less in demand and more anonymous. When I finally let go of my fantasy and left this ill-conceived excursion after too many months, I realized my own suffering. Undeniably I had taken the wrong path. But I have tried to learn from it and accept that "the wind was contrary" (Matt. 14:24, KJV).

I was trying to integrate my sexual side with the rest of my personality. But by choosing a one-dimensional endeavor, I aggravated the problem. I also discovered that I was not alone, for our society cultivates pure sexuality without regard to its relationship to values and ideas. What the fashion world expresses in hyperbole, the rest of advertising and entertainment expresses in modified form. Pure sexuality sells products, and male sexuality is most commonly displayed when it bears no relationship to a man's inner life. For too many of us, male sexuality is a highway sign with a giant-size replica of a cowboy smoking his way to oblivion.

*Sexuality and the Soul*

My episode in modeling has influenced the way I think about how men are portrayed and the sexual values they grow up with. It's also been an eye-opener for me about my own psychology of sexuality and the soul.

That ill-conceived experience has reminded me that, like many men, I have a hard time focusing on my own sexuality. It is much easier and more natural for me to concentrate on women than to think about the sexual energy I'm expressing. Given the choice, I'd much prefer to stare at a comely woman than spend similar time considering my own body or what I'm wearing. But there is something spiritually disconcerting about that, since it involves a good deal of self-negation and denial. Unless I can comfortably embrace all sides of myself, including the spiritual and the sexual, wholeness is impossible.

In a way, I pursued the modeling opportunity to confront my internal dilemma. I tried desperately to focus on my sexuality through doing something exclusively physical. I wanted to prove something to myself and dramatically change a part of my existence. Perhaps subconsciously, I wanted people to focus on me physically instead of intellectually. But my sense of direction and my choices were unquestionably wrong.

Instead of considering sexuality thoughtfully, I found a preoccupation that could provide only limited self-insight. Looking for a sense of fulfillment, I unconsciously sought acceptance and approval from women in particular. I wanted them to focus on me.

Until that period of my life, I had not fully experienced the sense of hurt and injury I carried with me about my sexuality. Was I masculine enough? Was I attractive enough? These insecurities haunted me and led to my course of action. Was it a characteristically male sense of injury? I believe so. A solid sense of confirmation was not there for me as a child. Despite some hard-fought gains in self-esteem made in my late teens and early twenties, the thirst for an indisputable sense of masculinity remained. I felt the need for repairs, but I was driving in the wrong direction for help. As the wise man said, "there are many devices in a man's heart" (Prov. 19:21, KJV).

It is now apparent to me that people can gain lasting self-worth only through coming to terms with themselves, not through outside affirmation or acclaim. When the applause dies down or the young admirers fail to stare, a person is left alone to be with himself. For men who feel hurt or frustration concerning sexuality, aloneness can be a frightening ordeal. Sexuality is for men the most vulnerable of areas, and acknowledging anguish or fear is a lot like a sharp pain in your groin.

"Damn, it hurts!" you say to yourself. But time after time you must unveil your wounded sexual ego and take it into the world. Despite the odds against change, a man must build his self-esteem from the inside. He must conquer self-doubt not with the sword of mindless bravado, but with the grace of insight and personal respect.

Following the modeling episode, I uncovered a deep layer of anger about sexuality. While pretending to accommodate the rigidly defined roles for men in advertising, or for men in society overall, I resented expectations that reflected only a narrow thimble of life. My own experiences seemed much richer than the roles and moods I was being asked to create ("the boyish look"; "the serious look").

Could that be true for men in everyday life? I wondered. My anger took form in disliking most prescribed notions of manhood and electing to write about my experiences. But anger, too, has its limitations. When a person harbors anger, a sense of peace about sexuality is impossible. The deepest masculine sexual experience is effortless and upbeat, not shackled by old angers and vigilance.

It has taken some time, but I have come to believe that integration of the sexual and the soulful is possible for me, and for other men as well. I can't prove that, but I feel it in a way that means more to me than verifiable proof. Our world is terribly specialized; everybody seems proficient at some things, and no one seems comfortable with everything. That reality makes psychological wholeness difficult, but it can be achieved. Over the last few years, the most pressing question for me has been: "How can I bring these apparently separate sides of myself together and end the war inside of me?"

The only answer that has made sense for me is: I must find a true spirituality beyond the way I have conventionally thought about the soul. I must find a spirituality that does not minimize male sexuality, but accounts for it in a most compelling and personally meaningful way. Seeking that vision of the soul, I look within, while allowing my journey to be informed by the views of other men and the sociology of our times with regard to male sexuality.

### The Sexual Struggles of Men

"How do you learn about sex? I remember being in grade school, and the big thing was a picture of Bill Russell and some other basketball stars in a topless bar. I think it was in *Sports Illustrated* and it got passed around. The librarian clipped the picture out of the magazine. That was a big deal;

it made the thing seem even more like a taboo." Those were the words of Bill, a thirty-one-year-old fellow, speaking about male sexuality. Like many other men, Bill concentrated on sexual women and could recall virtually no organized learning about sexuality.

Men learn about sex and sexuality in all kinds of ways, but few seem to discuss the subject with their fathers or with other adults. Male sexuality rarely serves as a subject for talks, and when it does, it is typified more by anxiety than open exchange. Sexuality is not addressed as part of a larger developmental personal picture.

Many men express a comfort with sexuality only in aggressive ways. Without realizing it, we acquire an aggressive sexuality. We believe the best way to be sexual is to assert ourselves in a bullyish manner, without regard to the feelings of anyone who might be affected. Men picture male sexuality in "rough and ready" terms and show little flexibility in our approaches to women. We let mercy and truth forsake us (Prov. 3:3, KJV).

Those of us who so hyperaggressively view sexuality will not have access to our tender sides and to our tender passions. Our capacity for sexual experience is therefore blocked. Some men don't even recognize their softer side, let alone put that side into practice. Tender sexuality is, then, considered unmanly and makes little sense throughout our young adult and middle adult years.

Aggressive sexuality has no soul. What moral lessons does it pass on to future generations of little boys? There is little value in the fusion of sex and aggression, for it demands that men be one-dimensional, limited, and selfish. It precludes a man from rounding out his personality and living up to his religious ideals.

"I used to be real simple, just go at it sexually and not get committed," said twenty-six-year-old Bart. "But I got the feeling I was kidding myself. Where was I going? I guess you could say I took a look at myself and figured I could use a touch-up. But most of all, I just looked at my habits in practical terms and saw I was treating women pretty badly. I figured my relations would be better if I cooled it."

When it comes to aggression and sexuality, change is a difficult and threatening thing for many men. Schooled in the lessons of bravado, many men fear relinquishing entrenched forms of behavior. Younger men may be growing up in a postfeminist era, but their resolve about sexual aggression may be no different from their fathers. As if it reflected male sexuality in its entirety, the sexual-aggressive ethos seems to traverse generational differences, though it is most vivid in the young. "Youth, with a whole life before it, can make serious mistakes" (Eccles. 11:10).

The emphasis on sex and aggression reflects a deep, abiding insecurity about manliness among men. Aggression emerges not when a person feels powerful, but when he doubts his power. We use aggression when we are not sure we can control someone sexually.

Insecurity is another common theme that I have witnessed among men. Many of us are overly defensive and guarded when it comes to sexual habits. We even develop a certain vigilance about intimate sexual questions. With sexuality, the ground we walk on just doesn't seem that firm. We anchor ourselves with popular notions of manhood, especially the aggressive sexual stance, and try to feign security. But our security is a charade; deep down we live in fear of inadequacy.

"Sex?" exclaimed thirty-five-year-old Rico. "The only thing that matters is whether you're getting enough lately. Give me a break!"

"Talking about sex," says forty-seven-year-old Mike, an apartment house manager, "is a lot of crap. It's action that counts. I don't go in for that Dr. Ruth garbage. I think men talk with their deeds, not with a lot of BS. I don't really have anything to say about it, because it's not anybody else's business. If I had nothing better to do than talk about sex, then my life would be pretty dull. No offense, but I think it's a stupid idea to worry about men's sexuality."

Mike and Rico are far from unusual in their cut-and-dried attitude. Many men reject thinking about themselves introspectively, as if male sexuality were a plague or a curse. The fears in Mike's voice, for example, were apparent as he deflected even unobtrusive questions. It is not just the fear of inadequacy that motivates men like Mike to avoid or denounce talk of sexuality, it is also the fear of discovery. Mike is afraid of parts of himself that he does not recognize or understand—parts of himself that belong with his sexuality and could make him a fuller and more satisfied person. Mike is as frightened of his soul as he is protective of his penis, for the soul is something he cannot control or manipulate.

The soul is whole, and men like Mike are not prepared for wholeness; personal integration does not make sense to them. Wholeness is counter to the world of divisions, compartments, functions, and levels that men like Mike feel comfortable with. They would rather be safe and secure, splitting life down the middle between the good ideas and the bad ideas. But life is more complex than that, for "God's ways are as mysterious . . . as the wind" (Eccles. 11:5).

I've sensed another troublesome attitude among many men. In the same way that men see themselves in divided terms, as if we could easily be categorized or as if parts of our personalities were unrelated to each other, we view women in segmented ways. This phenomenon is sometimes called the "Madonna/Whore Complex." It's a means by which men try to organize their own sexuality and sort out women, but it keeps men from a thorough appreciation of women and of their own potential for relating.

Those of us who imagine women in a Madonna/Whore way conjure a twofold sexual world. We believe women fall into two categories: asexual or wickedly sexual. We picture only these two types.

"Basically, you got two kinds of women," explained thirty-nine-year-old Mack, a surveyor. "You got your nice kind and your not-so-nice kind. When you're young, all the guys like the sexy kind. But when you're starting to get old like me, that all changes."

The Madonna aspect of our imagery usually relates to our ideas about virtue and the maternal role. When we see a woman as a Madonna type, we unconsciously equate her with repression. We may think of her inner qualities and see her as a good mother and a reliable wife. We may associate her with security and substance, but not attraction or excitement. If we depict a woman as a Madonna, we might marry her, but we would not take her to the senior prom, select her as cheerleader, identify her as Miss Universe material, or imagine being with her in a romantic setting. She is not the type of girl the Beach Boys sang about, nor would she fit neatly into our fantasy lives.

In contrast, we relegate other women to the status of the Whore. We see some women as ostentatiously sexual and glittery, lacking substance almost by definition. Although we may gravitate toward such women or pull away from them with trepidation, we generally see them as evil and selfish, perhaps even narcissistic. Thoughts of these women are blatantly sexual, and they seem to go hand in hand with our wilder sides. Our ideas about these women seem antithetical to religion and to our basic values. They appear dangerous and exotic, and that is part of the appeal. We want to be seen with them. They are perfect for carefree sex, a fling, or extramarital affairs, but we would not get close to them in any serious or enduring way. They seem untrustworthy. They represent heat but not warmth. They are the inspiration for sex-filled movies and magazine advertisements—the luscious, seductive figures of our fantasies.

Those who divide women in this manner cannot relate to a whole woman. Of course, no woman is really one type or the other, but these are the stereotypes we impose on women. The successful merging of these images is necessary for sexual fulfillment—for both men and women.

Daniel, age thirty-nine and single, spoke about what he sees among his single counterparts, both male and female. "People either are looking for someone to be a parent or for a one-nighter. That's the big problem. It's hard to find someone to have an adult relationship with. Either the women and the guys came dressed like the Happy Hooker and Richard Gere, or they look old enough to have teen-age kids and are looking for someone to play mother or father to their kids. I keep looking for someone in between, and I've been looking since I was divorced nine years ago, but I just keep being frustrated. Maybe it's the way of the world, maybe not."

*Why Is Sexuality Such a Collective Problem?*
Even after the sexual revolution of the 1960s, few parents socialize their children about sexuality the way they do about religion or politics. Their neglect leaves us open to the teachings of the television and entertainment industries, which bombard children with a whole host of ideas about gender and sexuality, especially through their advertisements. "Sin . . . is written with . . . the point of a diamond" (Jer. 17:1, KJV).

"It bothers me the way sex is for sale every night on television," comments George, a fifty-two-year-old merchant. "The commercials are getting to be all the same thing, and they don't care about all the little kids watching them. A lot of the women are half-naked."

Fashion advertising suggests what gender roles are popular and acceptable. They tell us how to act with a beer can in our hands and how to treat women when we wear a popular cologne. Gender and sexuality are such pivotal cornerstones in this world that David Ogilvy, cofounder of the highly successful advertising agency of Ogilvy and Mather, once offered the sweeping statement: "When you use photographs of a man in advertising, you exclude women from the audience."

When advertising highlights superficiality and materialism, it trivializes male sexuality and crams it into a few tightly conceived images. Clothing and accoutrements are forms of self-expression, and even sexual self-expression, but the "right" clothing does not constitute a good man or a good sexual man. Sexuality is a matter of inner qualities put forth in mind and heart. Outward appearance, then, can be only a facsimile of those qualities, but too often in our society it masquerades as the truth itself. When we choose to covet, it is smart to covet "the best [and truest] gifts" (1 Cor. 12:31, KJV).

"I guess when I think about sexuality," commented twenty-three-year-old Andy, a restaurant host, "I think about dressing up for a date and looking really good. I think of driving a sports car and going to a disco. Letting loose for a fine-looking woman. And doing it in style. That's what sexy means to me."

"A big part of being sexy is how much money you make and how much power you have," says twenty-nine-year-old Curtis, a commercial real estate agent. "I mean, no girl wants to go out with a stiff!"

Advertising and commercial imagery are an insidious part of our lives, and they very much affect the way we see ourselves sexually. But advertising does an injustice when it tries to define the good life as the material aspects of a man's life. Such advertisements encourage men to focus on appearances. By implication, it discourages men from looking inward.

One of the prevailing motifs in modern advertising aimed at men is sexual courage. Trend-setting commercials and pictures depict men acting confidently in a sexual manner, in regard either to some natural challenge, like mountain climbing, or that unpredictable human challenge—a woman. But advertising does not ask men to be bold and unique; it beseeches men to conform and be part of the herd of other men who use the designated product. Is conformist behavior sexy?

The success of any product depends on the majority of men "going along" and not standing out from the crowd.

Manufacturers have a need for men to adhere to a thin standard of sexuality, and we oblige too willingly, sacrificing the individuality that can actually open up our sexuality.

Fashion critic Anne Hollander said of this tendency: "The need for constant impact naturally causes originality to get confused with the capacity to cause a sensation; and sensation can always be created, just as in all show business, by the crudest of illusions."

The other fundamental theme that advertising perpetuates is the vain "machismo man." The typical scenario is a confident, severe-looking fellow with rippling muscles and imposing size telling men to buy brake liner fluid or fashion underwear. Whether or not the male model is well-known or anonymous, whether he's a Chicago Bear or an auto mechanic, the body language reveals the message. "Buy this product if you want to be a man!" But with such a preponderance of "weight room" advertisements, the expression of inner sexuality and tender sexuality goes by the billboard. Advertisements rarely get beyond machismo; they hold men hostage. We are suspended in time, unable to do anything sexual but conquer challenges with the aid of a commercial product.

The sexual themes of conformism and machismo do indeed dominate popular cultural advertising and influence our perceptions. That's one of the main points of *Sex Stereotyping in Advertising,* a book by researchers Alice Courtney and Thomas Whipple. In one of the most comprehensive studies done of magazine advertising over an extended period, the researchers found a clear and alarming pattern. Men and women are both pictured sexually as mere objects by most magazines, and sexual teasing or stripping is a common activity. It is not clothing that is really emphasized, but the removal of clothing.

According to these researchers, men are commonly depicted as sexual world beaters who lack sensitivity and other human sexual qualities. Men are rarely seen in an array of real-life situations and are rarely cast with children, and never with elderly men or women. Courtney and Whipple conclude: "The studies indicate that men and women are indeed shown stereotypically in advertising in general-interest magazines, and that over a twenty-year period there have been only minor changes."

Nineteen-year-old Pete, a college sophomore, noticed the phenomenon and described it in his own words. "Too many girls I know look at *GQ* or *M* and think that's the way guys should be. They expect guys to be neat, tough, and perfect. Who could measure up to that? It pisses me off. I guess we do the same to girls. But one thing I've learned at college is you have to leave all these silly, dreamy ideas behind."

*How Can We Make Sexuality More Spiritual?*

I believe that the most difficult psychological task for men is to integrate the sexual and the spiritual, eros and spirit. We live in a world that increasingly separates the two in a clear and pronounced way. The cues we receive from popular culture and from our friends and relatives suggest a world where sex and soulfulness don't mix. But we must accept the challenge and ask ourselves: "How can we create a more spiritual sexuality for ourselves?" As with the rest of life, God is the answer.

Through my own experiences, both painful and rewarding, I've learned a number of things about my ability to integrate these separate sides of myself. As a result of a few personal discoveries, I see my own sexuality and the sexuality of other men a bit differently. I believe that today I have a better vision of healthy male sexuality, and a clearer idea of how a person can blend sex and soulfulness. I also believe that God wants me to be happy and fulfilled.

Above all, I've learned that a man must know himself sexually beyond the "grunt" and "feel good" stage. We have to transcend popular cultural notions of manhood and deal with sexual realities. We have to consider not only what gives us pleasure and what doesn't, but why. We need to understand who and what attracts us, always keeping in mind what is good for our whole beings. We must treat our bodies with respect and spirituality.

What are my sexual strengths and weaknesses? What are my worst fears about sexuality? We must have the courage to ask these questions. By considering these and similar questions, we can approach a greater honesty—and candor is always the main highway leading to the dominion of the soul.

Integration demands that we cease doing some things that are troublesome, too. As thoughtful men, we must stop viewing sex as raw, impulsive, and valueless; at the same time we must stop thinking of tranquillity and the spirit as either nonexistent or nonsexual. The soul exists and it is sexual: sex *is* a spiritual word. We must come to accept that notion and embrace it. Only through that awareness can we appreciate the depth in women and in ourselves. Only through that belief can we come to grips with a personalized God who has meaning for us as men. Ultimately that must be a God who includes our sexuality—a decidedly male sexuality—in that

Deity's infinite design; a God who "taketh pleasure in his people" (Ps. 149:4, KJV).

Finally, it is imperative that we concentrate on a view of sexuality that can be truly gratifying. We must etch into our lives the reality that only sexuality inspired by love is fulfilling, that erotic sexuality, or even nurturant sexuality alone, can never be sufficient. Only male sexuality filled with the richness of love will do. We need to focus upon that as the center of our sexual lives—breathe it, cultivate it, and sleep with it. If we wish to reach our sexual potential, we must allow loving sexuality to become part of us.

I would urge you to strive toward that goal and tie it to your notions of manhood. It can move the trials and misadventures of your life to an unexplored plane of existence. It can free you to live your masculinity, not just speak about it. After all else is said and done, a comfort with masculine love is what brings us the greatest satisfaction.

"I want to fall in love," says twenty-one-year-old Danny. "That's really what matters to me most. I know that's what makes you happy."

All of us wrestle with that wish. As men, it is our ability to love that guides our sexuality and offers us a home for our passions. Step by step, we learn the great relationship lesson that meaningful sex is indeed a very spiritual thing. Our lives can only be richer for this important discovery.

# CHAPTER 9

# ROMANCING
# THE SOUL

*For the winter is past, the rain is over and gone . . . the
time of the singing of the birds has come.*
*—Song of Sol. 2:11*

For many men, finding a partner for life is one of the most
compelling desires. But where does a man find someone to
love and be loved by? That question is as old as the history
of dating, and the possible answers are as varied as anyone's
potential marital partners. Sometimes we find these answers
in the strangest places—like just around the corner.

In the spring of 1986 I moved to Boston and settled into
a new apartment, eager to begin the next phase of my life in
a city I had loved when I was at Harvard. I was excited about
moving back, and perhaps more open than usual to new
experiences. Perhaps deep down I knew that this was "a time
for loving" (Eccles. 3:8).

On the first Saturday afternoon following my move—the
date was August 9—I strolled unassumingly into the
7-Eleven on Charles Street in Beacon Hill. It was a bright but

humid day, and I stopped for some juice or a soft drink—whatever struck me once I reached the refrigerated area of the store. I decided to go with something different—Very-Fine papaya juice. In addition to the juice, however, I found something else and someone else that was very different.

"At least I get to talk to you," the woman behind the cash register blurted as she apologized for not having change for my twenty-dollar bill. I was momentarily startled by her friendliness.

"That's okay," I offered in response to her apologies.

I discovered that her name was Elizabeth, and that she was twenty-two and had just graduated from Santa Clara University in California. She was a "California Girl" by birth but had lived in Illinois, Florida, Louisiana, and Georgia before returning to California for college. I concluded that her frequent moves helped account for a certain precocious maturity.

Elizabeth learned that I was twenty-eight, which didn't seem to faze her. She was pleased that I was new to Boston, just as she was. She had arrived just five days before. Our chat ended with warmth and smiles, and I said I would be in to visit.

It wasn't long before I asked Elizabeth to dinner. Our first date was full and adventuresome; coincidentally we wore the same colors that night, and our oneness continued on through the evening. We shared a plate of pasta at the Harvard Bookstore Café, a romantic walk to the waterfront, and dessert in the Italian North End of Boston. We also shared open and exuberant conversation. Each of us was eager to know about the other and to tell the experiences that had brought us to this point in our lives. The only physical contact that evening was a very warm hug good night. I will always smile when I remember that hug and the deep sense of friendship I carried home with me.

Open disclosure about ourselves and the world we saw around us characterized our early dates. Our conversations were not lofty, but came from deep within our hearts. We both strove for honesty and closeness, though sometimes fear or guilt about pleasure interrupted the growing intimacy between us. We exchanged books and poetry, and shared our ideas and dreams. We were allowing each other into our hearts.

As Elizabeth and I settled into our relationship, events and emotions developed in a rapid, almost relentless fashion. It was like a stream running toward the ocean, with God's hand guiding the way. But when the stream became a whirling rapid, we felt hurled together in a closeness we weren't always prepared for. Yet a force between us brought us beyond our fears, a force of great love and strength—one that could only be God's.

We had set forth on an irreversible course. I believe we wanted it that way. We were making a commitment to grow together unless that ran against God's wishes for us. All couples must make such a pact if they desire a relationship with depth. A relationship that places God at the center, one "filled with the fruits of righteousness" (Phil. 1:11).

"I can feel our growth and the depth between us, but it's scary sometimes," each of us would say as our relationship progressed. What was most scary was that we were venturing into the unknown, into a realm of love neither of us had known before. Indeed, we went through many, many crises of faith and doubt about our feelings, especially in our first year together. But during our doubting times we felt most vividly the presence of God's hand guiding our path. Faith in God gave us the strength to believe in the gift we had discovered—each other.

The sharing continued, with considerable discussion—often difficult—about parents, brothers, sisters, triumphs and disappointments and ambitions. We shared information and feelings, sometimes painfully but always fruitfully, as we became the hope chests for each other's life investments. It was as if we were trying to say to each other: "Seal me in your heart" (Song of Sol. 8:6).

Insecurities severely tested the middle period of our dating. Romanticized visions of the opposite sex and unreasonable expectations also troubled us. We had to overcome these obstacles, but relinquishing fantasies was painstaking work. Elizabeth and I worked hard at this, both as a couple and as individuals, for we began to realize that discovering the reality of each other was the only way to genuine satisfaction. No relationship can be healthy and enjoyable when past expectations dictate your lives. It is difficult to feel God's presence in another when we are focused on fantasy.

Elizabeth and I went through many personal trials early in our relationship. We survived the deaths of my grandfather and Elizabeth's grandmother and aunt, her unemployment and career selection angst, my roller coaster existence in writing, and any number of difficult confrontations, all within the first nine months of knowing each other. What was the glue that held us together? It could only be our faith and love for each other and God's gentle strength helping us through. God helped us "endure" (James 5:11).

Dealing openly with the dilemmas that faced us—both internal feelings and external events—we allowed our relationship to solidify around our mutual desire and human need for each other. We accepted that no person is self-sufficient and realized that complete and fulfilling love meant embracing the concept of total vulnerability to the other. "There is no fear in love" (1 John 4:18, KJV).

The "we-ness" of our lives began to take hold. The challenges that could have destroyed our feelings for each other only strengthened our bond. We survived each test and discovered a strange and wonderful inevitability about our relationship, an unshakable, irresistible love more compelling than we had ever imagined. We began to do more and more things with each other, and with each new adventure, discovered new things in common. Even when it hurt to be so close to another soul, it did not matter. We had each other to learn from and to love. Indeed, "many waters can not quench the flame of love" (Song of Sol. 8:7).

I believe that only God could have created the rich and deep relationship that Elizabeth and I share—though I also believe that such a relationship is accessible to everyone. Through the many challenging experiences we encountered, including our religious background and cultural differences, we put our faith in God's hands. Our faith became truth; no other explanation could account for the soul relationship we found growing in each other's hearts. The passion and love could only be a gift from God. The wedding feast was about to be prepared (Matt. 22:8).

Elizabeth and I were engaged at Plymouth Rock and married there on Thanksgiving weekend 1989. God has guided us thus far, and we have faith God will always be with us. But faith, like relationships, takes daily commitment. Though we try to live spiritually, it is not always easy. We are not perfect, and the spiritual path is rarely clear and straightforward. There is no road map toward God, and sometimes we have to go forward without a compass. Yet in the wilderness, the light of intimacy and growth is most often the brightest of all.

"Sometimes it all seems like a miracle," Elizabeth says. "I mean how we met in the 7-Eleven and how we got to know each other. But I know that we have worked really hard with what we were given, and that's something we must never lose—how much we value each other's company and love."

Making a soul relationship work requires the ability to experience all sides of life—the good, the bad, and the uncertain. Together, Elizabeth and I are participants and spiritual observers as our relationship deepens and changes. We have learned how a man and a woman can find their own souls and, in the process, find each other. We try to keep our eyes on the soulful path, a path that a person can see only with his or her heart. Love is what fulfills and sustains.

*The Trouble Men Have in Finding a Spiritual Relationship*

My own life experiences are particular to me, yet they illustrate some standard patterns for men. Few of us find a partner tailor-made for us. Instead, most men report that relationships require time and patience. A person takes his chances with love and hopes for the best.

Each of us brings to a relationship our own inner obstacles. During the last two years, I've spent considerable time thinking about my own attitudes about men and women and about the ideas of other men around me. I have found that many of us display characteristic patterns. Recognizing them in ourselves is no fun, but it's certainly preferable to suffering under their domination. Self-awareness is crucial to becoming a spiritual man.

Single men may exhibit these debilitating patterns more vividly, but married men show them with disturbing frequency. They interfere with a healthy relationship and with the full acceptance of our lovers and spouses. Men must assume responsibility for these patterns and match up their interpersonal lives with higher values and spiritual beliefs. We must love God with all our hearts, souls, and minds (Matt. 22:37).

*The Right One Pattern.* Those of us who are plagued by this view of relationships and of women believe only one person in the universe can satisfy our needs. We either search aimlessly for that mythical individual or we wait endlessly for that person to step into our lives. Because we are so certain that only this imagined person will do, we screen out other potential lovers and friends who don't fit our preconceived mate description. Consequently we shut out a good deal of life because we are looking in the wrong direction.

The seeds of the "right one pattern" can be found in a man who is tied to fantasy rather than reality. A man doesn't need to be crazy to evidence this pattern; he just needs to be a trifle neurotic. When our ideas about women and love are fueled by childhood experiences, popular culture, or peer influences, our vision of healthy romance is bound to be distorted. The image of the "right one" is invariably drawn from this constellation of factors and not from the soul. Its damage is subtle, but it can be persistent. Too many men who focus on "the right one" are lonely and frustrated for many years of their lives. It is hard for them to find "a virtuous woman" (Prov. 31:10, KJV).

Chuck, a train conductor, demonstrated some of this pattern, but he seems to be letting go of it. At age thirty-two,

Chuck wants more out of life than he has experienced. That desire has become a driving force for change in Chuck.

"I've always been a guy who wanted the best, particularly when it comes to women. It's not that I'm hard to get along with," Chuck continued, "it's just that I've always had a clear idea of what I wanted in a wife. Tall, slender, real classy-looking, with a real good sense of humor. I've met some nice girls over the years, but nobody seems to fit exactly what I'm looking for." Then, as an afterthought, Chuck offered: "I got to admit I'm getting kind of impatient. Lately I've been trying to think over what I want. We'll have to see . . . I'd just like to find someone to care for. Do you know what I mean?"

Men like Chuck often let go of their unreasonable expectations, but not till relationships have suffered. In a sense, time is their spiritual ally. The longer their fantasy persists and the more ungratifying it becomes, the more motivated they become to accept the reality of women in their lives—with their shortcomings as well as their capacity for love, too. These men are finally able to perceive and accept the humanness of women and allow genuine love into their lives.

*The Island Man Pattern.* A second pattern I have recognized in myself and in other men concerns the myth of total and unqualified self-sufficiency. The belief that we can take care of everything ourselves adversely affects the development of a satisfying soul relationship. When you convince yourself that you are completely satisfied alone, how can you recognize an enduring need for someone else?

The "island man" is often very good at many things, including his vocation. He likes to control situations and be the determining factor in any risk or gamble. Because of his mandate to establish his prowess, he has a hard time realizing and admiring the contributions of others. He is generally more self-absorbed than self-involved, a victim of interpersonal fear more than boundless ego. Quietly he asks himself, "Where is the place of my rest?" (Isa. 66:1, KJV)

In relationships, the "island man pattern" ironically renders this seemingly self-sufficient man helpless when it comes to opening up and disclosing himself. The emphasis on the facade of total sufficiency is too extensive for any genuine dropping of the guard. Because he cannot open up, he cannot be comfortable with others when they reveal intimate matters. He sees this as a sign of weakness or personal inadequacy. Although he may at first attract and welcome women who wish to rely on him, he will ultimately lose respect for them as a result of their dependency. In all relationships, he quickly establishes boundaries and protects them, even at the risk of losing a desired relationship.

"My former wife wanted too much from our marriage," said a disgruntled Kirk, age thirty-eight and a bartender. "It always seemed like she wanted to spend more time together than I did. She would have spent every free moment with me if she could. I cared about her, but I needed to get away from her to get anything done. I don't have any hard feelings, but I doubt whether I would get married again."

*The Prehistoric Man Pattern.* Partly as a result of the value placed upon machismo by many societies, some men are prone to equate masculinity with raw aggression. Breast-beating is not truly masculine; such behavior is an exaggeration of traditional male traits. Beastlike qualities do not reflect men at their spiritual best. The beast in each of us must be tamed for satisfying relationships to develop.

For those who revere aggression, problems with women abound. The "prehistoric man pattern" beckons us to prove our virility at every turn, and the critical test is always physical in nature. We try incessantly to establish our dominance over other men, and over women, too. In romance, this primitiveness compels us to push for relations that are more like battles than tender romance. In fact, we can't tolerate our tender sides; the thought of such "weakness" makes us angry.

When men suffer from the prehistoric man pattern, they don't know how to take no for an answer, and they don't know how to say yes themselves. In other words, it is hard for them to be agreeable. There is something inherently oppositional in the prehistoric pattern, as if the afflicted man has somehow been wronged by life, or by his mother or father. In any case, their girlfriends and wives often bear the brunt of the abuse they levy. These men have lost sight of God's way.

Billy, age twenty-two and an auto mechanic, says it tersely when he lets you know what's on his mind. "I have no time for women who want a guy to play up to them and act like a gentleman. I'll take a girl any time who's got sex on her mind. I like it often and I like it hard. It's gonna be hard to find a woman who can tie me down."

With his rodeo metaphor, Billy accurately noted that it will be difficult to find a partner. Of course, for every Billy, there is a woman who subconsciously desires his abuse. But few women will want such a relationship for a lifetime. With an attitude toward sex and toward women like Billy's, a man cannot get close to a mature woman. Whatever Billy's hurts and fears, and however deep-seated they are, it would be difficult for anyone to empathize and help him, even if he were to let anyone get that close.

The "prehistoric man pattern" protects men from closeness and from self-awareness. It keeps us from spiritual matters because it refuses to recognize that spirituality exists. Ironically it is denial, which decades ago was considered a feminine tendency, that keeps these men from real relationships and deeper satisfaction. But an honest outlook, not denial, readies us for God.

*The Don't Rock the Boat Pattern.* Some of us don't like to take chances. Our lives and our relationships are characterized by order and sameness. We don't like to do or say anything that makes us tense, even falling in love or professing deep faith.

Those of us who want life to be "steady as she goes" try to arrange our lives in a tight and narrow fashion. While we may be highly capable of sustaining relationships and even marriage, our relations lack intimacy, spontaneity, and excitement. But we need these qualities. We may even seek a partner with a similar psychological and spiritual disposition. Together we collude in choosing not to grow. We may not fight and we may not be lonely, but fulfillment is foreign to us.

"I think people want too much out of marriage these days," said forty-year-old Ernie, a dentist who has been married for ten years. "Too many of my friends still think it should be exciting all the time. 'When are you going to grow up?' I say to them in not so many words. Marriage is a contract that people enter into because they want to have children and pass along a tradition. I think that it really doesn't matter that much who you marry, as long as you learn to get along. Then you try to go through the years without a lot of stress and bring your kids up in a safe environment," Ernie concluded.

Most "don't rock the boat" men are easy for others to accept and do not appear to be especially unhappy. But neither do they appear to be buoyant. Their lives are consistent and predictable. When a sudden change occurs, like illness or other misfortune, they have a particularly difficult time. The sameness of their lives makes it very hard for them to change. In spiritual terms, their notion of God is static, so religious fervor and heartfelt investments are unlikely.

These four patterns of relating, "the right one," "the island man," "the prehistoric man," and "don't rock the boat," are only four of the many patterns that adult men demonstrate when it comes to dating and marital relations. Yet these patterns are distinguished by their frequency. Each of these patterns clouds our path toward the love of others, and the love of God as well.

For those of us troubled by these problems, our fundamental challenge is to break free of these patterns and open up ourselves to things that are refreshing and unique. The key word in this process is change. We must be willing to see change as our ally and as God's instrument, not as a threat. A typical process for an individual man might go something like this: (1) recognize and accept the troublesome pattern, (2) monitor its appearance in our relations, and (3) keep even closer watch over it and discipline ourselves to stop thinking and acting in that manner. If we can conquer that debilitating pattern, a more satisfying life-style will naturally emerge. We will learn to act comfortably in our relationships, balancing self-interest with love for a spouse or girlfriend. We will feel more deeply masculine inside, too, for a sense of wholeness will give us the confidence to explore greater depth in our relationships. That is God's method of healing, but we must accept it so it can work for us. "Grace be with those that love the Lord" (Eph. 6:24).

When you relate to other people, particularly partners or potential partners, you must reject any pulls toward your old self-defeating pattern. Tell others that you don't want any part of those patterns. Be persistent yet patient. Change may scare them. You need to balance letting someone else change without compromising your own desire to change. It can be a delicate chore sometimes, but it's a necessary act for spiritual partnership.

*What Does Your Relationship Have to Do with God?*

Most men can appreciate that psychological problems can interfere with a relationship more easily than they can see these dilemmas as matters of the spirit. Whether or not you suffer from any of these patterns, you may wonder what your relationships have to do with God. Particularly if you are not religious, you may have asked: "Does God have anything at all to do with what I share with my lover?"

Through my experiences with Elizabeth I have discovered that no soul relationship is possible without God—even if you don't at first recognize the presence of God. Without God's guidance and direction, I could not have met Elizabeth. But even more important, neither of us would have had the vision or the strength to pursue the apparent compatibility between us. Neither of us could have endured the trials of our growing closeness without God's love watching over us, and like a true friend God loved us at all times (Prov. 17:17).

Without our faith in God, our background differences would have been insurmountable. We could not have tolerated the tension of other people's judgments and our own doubts. Without God, any relationship has its problems. With God, all types of relationships are possible. Gradually we learned that basic maxim, and we have tried to make it a central part of our lives.

The process of finding God in a relationship is difficult to describe. Yet, despite their having a certain ineffability, I want to leave you with a few of the spiritual lessons I have learned through my experiences. I encourage you to list for yourself the many ways God may emerge in your relationship. You might ask your wife, friend, or lover to join you in this spiritual task and then discuss what you've found. Here are some ways you might consider:

*Romancing the Soul: God's Presence in a Relationship*

1. God is in both of you each and every day. God is there when you care for and accept each other, even when it is difficult.

2. God exists in your secure sense of manhood and in your lover's confident femininity, and especially in the way the two blend together.

3. God was there in the uncanny circumstances under which you met, and in the sustaining force of your relationship.

4. God is there when you stay together against all odds and you are both glad you did. This is "faith which worketh by love" (Gal. 5:6, KJV).

5. God is in the convergence of your experiences earlier in life, given greater meaning by the reality of an enduring relationship. "Rejoice, O young man, in thy youth" (Eccles. 11:9, KJV).

6. God is in your desire for children, or God exists in the loving presence of your children.

DAVID HELLER

7. God lives in your warm, comforting feelings; God breathes in your fiery passions.

8. God is the warmth in winter that your relationship provides, and the cool shade in summer, too.

9. God is in the depth of your conversations and mutual openness; God walks with you during each personal risk you take with each other.

10. God is the sense of home you create together, a home that transcends your house and material possessions. God is the eternal Home that awaits each of you.

11. God emerges in your mutual admiration and un-flinching respect for each other.

12. God is the inspiration behind your words when you say: "I am my beloved's and my beloved is mine" (Song of Sol. 6:3).

13. God speaks when you say to your beloved, "I am sorry," and when she answers back, "I forgive you."

14. God helps you have faith in your beloved when she and everyone else lose faith.

15. God moves you and your lover to share your love with the world. "Come, my beloved, let us go out into the fields and stay in the villages" (Song of Sol. 7:11). God is everywhere that two shall be as one.

# CHAPTER 10

# MEN AND CHILDREN

**D**ear God," writes ten-year-old Bruce, "how does it feel to be the biggest, best dad in the whole United States? You must make out okay on Father's Day."

The subject of children is close to my heart. I've devoted a good deal of my prior writing and research to the topic of children and religion, or more precisely, children's views of God. Several of my previous books, including *Dear God, What Religion Were the Dinosaurs?* and *Dear God: Children's Letters to God,* have concentrated on this very topic. From my interviews with boys and girls from a variety of religious backgrounds, I know that youngsters do commit to spiritual acts and beliefs. We adults should take their ideas very seriously and appreciate their heartfelt efforts at faith.

The media, both secular and religious, seem to be attracted to the universal message that children convey through their lovely innocence. Children carry with them a sense of God's constancy and love, and this makes for an interesting story indeed.

Yet some in the media report the topic with great ambivalence, or even worse, with a need to distort and sell. Sometimes they show little respect for either the sweetness of children or the sanctity of God.

Media portrayals of children and religion remind me of the disparate attitudes men in particular have about children. "The spiritual man has insight into everything and that bothers and baffles the man of the world" (1 Cor. 2:15).

In the winter of 1986, I received a phone call from a producer representing ABC's "20/20" show, who was interested in doing a segment based on my work with children. She asked for my help. Without much second thought, I agreed.

From my first visit to their studio, I should have sensed something was awry. The general atmosphere was superficial and phony. The producers spent more time in self-congratulatory talk than in genuine interaction. A week earlier they had covered the *Challenger* shuttle disaster, but their conversation revealed little feeling for the tragedy. They spoke mostly about their own coverage of it. I sensed that ratings, not caring for people or ideas, was the raison d'être of that studio.

"Wasn't it great the way we interviewed those kids right after the *Challenger* exploded?" a senior producer boasted to me.

The senior producer made me feel that some vital aspect of humanity was missing from this high-powered scene. His callous attitude toward the children in his segments was also an ominous harbinger of things to come. "They are blind and confused. Their closed hearts are full of darkness; they are far away from the life of God because they have shut their minds against him, and they cannot understand his ways" (Eph. 4:18).

When the time came to film my interviews with children, the crew moved to the classroom setting. The "20/20" personnel had little respect for the spontaneity and realism of the school we visited; and they tried to shape principal, teachers, and children to fit their own needs. Using the innocent excitement of the children, they tried to produce the kind of program and effect they wanted.

John, a distant and self-absorbed man in his early thirties, was the reporter assigned to the children-and-religion television segment. John's behavior throughout the videotaping was indicative of the entire crew, who treated the children like objects rather than people.

John always arrived late and left early. Whenever he was involved, he insisted that the entire production revolve around his own wishes. He showed little interest in or knowledge of the subject of the segment—God, and children's views of God. Instead, he had the cameras focused on what mattered to him most, his own profile.

Most troubling was John's relationship to the children. He ignored them unless he wanted a response from them. Then he promised them something for their cooperation. He pushed away the little boys and girls when they wanted autographs and often interrupted them when they spoke. He showed no respect for their individuality; he treated them as a group of objects that might be able to deliver what he was looking for—a segment that would make John look good. The subject of God and children was unapproachable for John, a self-proclaimed atheist. The combination of topic and reporter was an ironic and inexplicable match.

"How can I get those kids to talk?" he asked me. "They just seem like a dense group," he answered, revealing his callousness and insensitivity.

The results of John's misguided approach and the "20/20" crew's rudeness were not known to me until the segment aired in April of 1986. I felt a great mixture of rage and sadness as I saw John appear to interview some children I know he never met. I had actually conducted the interviews with these children, not he. I was dismayed to see the children's religious responses edited out to suit the more "scientific" approach of the television show. And the children's spontaneous ideas were cut short or distorted, thereby misleading the audience. Yet even more disturbing was the ill-treatment of a little nine-year-old girl, who specifically asked that her letter to God about her parents' marital problems not be read on television. But at the end of the segment, there was John lurking in the shadows of a churchlike edifice, reading the little girl's letter to a national audience. He stated that some of the kids didn't want their letters read on television, but that he was going to read them anyway because *he* deemed it appropriate.

The incident is a reminder in exaggerated fashion of how much power adults can wield over children, and how badly and belligerently that power can be applied. It beckons us to consider how we treat children, for the spiritual meaning of childhood is very important—not only for the youngsters, but also for men who are in search of their souls.

*The Everyday Habits of Fathers*

Fortunately, few men are as thoughtless with their own children as John and his television cohorts were with the children in the segment. Most fathers would shudder at the notion of pushing their children away or compromising their children's interests. Yet we do fall victim to more subtle negligence, even though we try hard to be caring fathers.

"I try every day to concentrate more on my children, think about their needs and interests. Also, about how they must picture me. But making a living and providing for them has to be my first concern. And it's a dominant worry. Sometimes it just doesn't leave any time for the other things you'd like to provide for your kids."

Those words spoken by Terry, a thirty-five-year-old father of two, describe a common dilemma for men in their efforts at fathering. How is it possible to accomplish all of the tasks of fatherhood?

Most of us initially see parenting as something to share equally with our wives. Particularly when our children are young, five years old or under, most of us are extremely dedicated to fathering in all of its dimensions.

But then something happens. As we and our children grow older, it becomes harder for us to keep up with the competing demands of work and family life. We shy away from the complexities of parenting, leaving the business of guidance to our wives and to the educational system. Throughout, we sense that we are missing out on something.

Albert, a forty-five-year-old postal worker, looked back on his children's upbringing: "I don't know where I was. I had to travel a lot when my kids started school, and before

I stopped traveling, they were in college. I find it difficult to replace the years, but the sad truth is, you can't replace them."

Constantine, a forty-year-old administrator, shares his own experiences: "It's so hard to spend enough time with your kids. But you got to. You get caught up in the rat race and forget what you're doing it all for."

We fulfill certain paternal functions by offering to our children what is most conventional, a breadwinning father. We may also serve as disciplinarians and role models, suggesting to them through our example that hard work pays off. Yet some aspects of our paternal role are left largely unfulfilled.

When Isaac bestowed his blessings on Esau and Jacob, his blindness made it impossible to tell the two brothers apart. In modern times, we are sometimes blind to the social and emotional needs of our children. So we sometimes neglect these areas of fathering.

One important quality that all children need from their fathers, boys as well as girls, is gentleness. "The fruit of the spirit . . . is gentleness" (Gal. 5:22). Yet that capacity for gentleness eludes us. We don't develop that quality as easily as we do aggressiveness or control. Why is that?

First, we believe gentleness to be sissified or unmanly. It's okay for women and maybe for children, but not for us. Second, gentleness goes against the grain of popular versions of manhood. We just don't have the time, or the flexibility, to slow down and be gentle. Next, we are afraid of the mystery of gentleness and its close ally, play. They are hard to categorize or reduce to an organized set of expectations. They involve a quality of letting go which is difficult for us to allow. And they involve the gentler side of a man's personality. "The servant of the Lord must . . . be gentle" (2 Tim. 2:24, KJV).

Patience is another characteristic that troubles us. "I come home every day exhausted and kind of a nervous wreck, especially when it's my turn to pick up my daughter from day care," said twenty-eight-year-old Mark, a bank employee. "I often have to rush out of work so I'm not late. When I get there she's all wound up to see me. The ride home is often frustrating. My mind is still on the office, and Susan talks and asks questions a mile a minute. I'm ready to scream by the time we get in the door. I wish I had more patience to sit down and play with her, but it's just not there. After a tough day at work, playing Barbies is the last thing I feel like doing."

Patience requires a capacity to see life in a proper time perspective. But too often our jobs skew that perspective with their emphasis on immediacy. Our hurried view of the world insidiously finds its way into our relationships with our children. We hurry our time with them, forgetting that they are not a business association but spiritual beings linked to us through love. And love, like all things that matter and last in life, takes time. Should a child be asked to grow up all at once?

In addition to gentleness and patience, we suffer from a lack of faith in our ability to nurture and love. Nurturant love is the first trait we look for in our wives; we are the *last* ones to claim it as our own. But our attitudes about nurturant love reveal a self-fulfilling and self-defeating prophecy: we assume that we are not loving, and therefore we are not all that we can be. But our assumption is false, for men have the same potential for love that women have. The Bible is full of examples of fathers who nurture their sons and daughters, but the trend in contemporary times is otherwise. Like David and Solomon, among others, it is our great mandate to love correctly, as a father to his son (Prov. 3:12).

My former college roommate, Dave, has worked very hard to develop his gentle, patient, and loving instincts. Dave is the father of two boys, Matthew (age six) and Michael (age four). With both of them, he demonstrates a steady attentiveness to their individual needs. He is not afraid to hug them, nor is he shy about setting reasonable limits, which are just as vital. I have been consistently impressed with how much energy he puts toward seeing things from his children's point of view. That ability, to momentarily assume the position of the child, is another special quality of fathering.

When I asked Dave about his secret of good fathering, he shrugged off my compliment and noted that he doesn't see his role in those terms. Quietly he acknowledged: "The boys have a lot of energy, and I try not to get in their way. I figure my role is to help guide them along with a little bit of discipline here and a lot of love there. I guess it's my Southern roots, but I see it as planting some seeds for the future. No use boasting about the harvest until it's full-grown!"

*How Can We Be Better Fathers?*

There is no easy solution to the mysteries of fatherhood. Each father and each of his sons and daughters is different. That uniqueness should always be recognized and respected. In fact, good fathering depends on the recognition of individual differences among children. Our unique personalities are one of God's greatest gifts to us, and "God's gifts and his call can never be withdrawn" (Rom. 11:29).

The soul needs to be part of everything we do as fathers.

From changing an infant's diapers to coaching a child's basketball team, each paternal act must be accompanied by the soulful caring of a father for his child. With each act, we must place God at the center of our relationships.

What does it mean to include God in our relationship to our children, just as Abraham did in his day?

We must remember how we experienced things as a child and apply that knowledge in our parental decisions. Family, school, and play are universal aspects of a child's life that transcend generational differences. Even though our children's lives appear different from our own as children, empathy, a special gift from God, can bridge the gap of father-child relationships.

"I think the most important thing is to remember what it was like when you were a kid," observed thirty-two-year-old Bryant, a bookstore employee. "That's one reason I think that 'Wonder Years' show is good for parents to watch—it helps you remember and see things from a little guy's shoes."

Our decision to have children is in itself a spiritual commitment. As in biblical times, today we still make a covenant with God when we have a child. Our part of the agreement is to nourish and care for the youngster in keeping with God's wishes. We can ask and anticipate that God will watch over that youngster, too. But we must adhere to our implicit promise—furnishing our youngster with the right values and home atmosphere. That responsibility requires more than just being a breadwinner; it demands a father present in the home and intimately involved in the lives of his children.

It may prove beneficial to ask yourself: "Am I really

involved in my son or daughter's life?" The answer may be complex, for it leads to the further issue of what parental involvement means. Involvement requires interest in the little things that concern your children, as well as in major things like food, clothing, and general welfare. Involvement means knowing how your child sees the world and even how he or she envisions God. A thoughtful father takes the time to ask his children about what God is like, and he also expresses his own ideas. He is prepared and eager for a spiritual dialogue with his children.

As men, we can also bear in mind that a healthy religious dialogue with our children is necessary for a fully developed sense of masculinity. Fathering can be a central aspect of masculine development, and spiritual fathering promises a richer masculine experience. A father-son relationship in particular is an exchange in which the emotions of masculinity will be at the forefront—not only for the son, but for his father as well.

Finally, it is good for a father to consider how he would like God to treat him. Perhaps you feel that God delivers for you, or maybe you doubt this. Assessing what you would like from God gives you a model of what your child may wish from you. It asks you to ponder how to be more like God with your child. To put it simply, how can you father your child in the spirit of God?

Work toward benign oversight with your child, and be inspired by a clear vision of God. Look inward for your gentleness and your love, and God will guide your destiny as a father. Place your hands in God's hands. God's gentleness will also make us better and more loving fathers.

*The Child in Each of Us*

Dear God,
    I think it is neat the way you get around so good
without a car. But you are still in so many places at
the same time. I heard that you are in every person.
In Dads and Moms and kids too. I hope that you are
in me a hole lot.

Love,
Mike (age eight)

Children write to God about all kinds of things, and more
often than not, their parents are a favorite subject. I have had
the good fortune to witness their originality and spontaneity
through my interviews, and it has been a great learning
experience for me.

Young Mike's letter reminds us that God is in all of us,
in parents as well as in children. But with his universal message, Mike inspires us to rediscover the child within each of
us—the little boy who yearns for God with steadfast faith. It
is the spirit of the child within that offers hope to us when
all else fails. It is the same spirit that sparks our important
aspirations—no matter how adult or distant from childhood
they may seem.

Recognizing the spirit of childhood, it is our solemn duty
as men to cultivate that spirit in our own children and to try
to maintain it ourselves. In concrete terms, that might mean
doing more childlike things with our children—for example,
making creative things, playing whiffle ball, riding bicycles,
or just climbing a tree together. The spirit of childhood can
transcend differences and friction and selfishness. It is a spirit
we must always treasure. Like a child's lamp beside his bed

as he sleeps, God's spirit, as expressed through children, shines through the night and provides light for all to share.

In helping our children to rekindle the spirit as their own, we must be wise enough to speak from our own hearts and minds. The only true father is a father who is genuine with his child. We must make God dear to us as fathers and pass along that spirituality to our children. We must father as we feel God fathers us, with loving kindness and respect.

# CHAPTER 11

# THE GREATEST
# MANHOOD
# OF ALL

**S**ome of the most valuable lessons I have learned in my life have come with the writing of this book on men and their souls. The lessons are not simple ones, but I believe they extend far beyond my small world. To write about male spirituality, I have had to explore the contours of my own masculinity. If done with a full heart, that undertaking will inevitably change a person. I know that I have been changed.

I began four years ago with little idea that the project would demand as much sweat and tears as it has. I didn't realize what it would mean to put my own manhood under a microscope and see what makes me tick. But I do now.

The book has accompanied me through several relationships and survived the rocky roads of publishing. Ultimately the book was accepted by a publisher that I had wished for but nearly given up on. The day before its acceptance I said to a friend that "it would take a miracle for the book to be accepted by this publisher." Indeed, it seems miracles do happen. "He heard me from heaven; my cry reached his ears" (Ps. 18:6).

Writing about men and spirituality, and then hearing how others react to this evocative subject, has been a rich and vital learning experience. The process of self-examination and sharing about masculinity can be overwhelming, but the rewards are valuable and enduring.

I have come to realize that God never abandoned me during my quest. I often felt that God demanded a great deal from me, yet God never let me settle for less than I was worthy of. Certainly I felt alone a good deal of the time as I wondered about the potency of my own masculinity and the fervency of my own faith. I wavered with self-doubt and skepticism about the fairness and orderliness of the world. But God was ever present, guiding my destiny while I retained brief glimpses of His presence.

I suspect that's the way it is for most men. God is not an obtrusive force that dominates our lives, but a subtle constant presence who remains unshakable even when we ourselves seem less sturdy.

I have also learned a good deal about what it means to have a masculine soul. To be aware of your soul means to live beyond gender and religious stereotypes and to treat yourself honestly. It means to believe that the essence of God is in you and works through you. In fact, you may well come to believe that your masculinity itself is a divine gift and that God works through you to accomplish His good intentions. To see ourselves as masculine instruments of God, yet wholly individual and free, is the great paradox for men, but "reverence for God gives us deep strength" (Prov. 14:26).

I have also become painfully cognizant of the obstacles to faith in the masculine soul. Our insecurities and fragile egos interfere with our ability to take in what God has to offer. We tend to travel in directions that keep us from greater personal truth. We rely on the false images of modern living, such as popular cultural icons, which obscure the vision of a God for all ages. These are our great adversaries, the most formidable hurdles we face in reclaiming our masculine souls.

Yet we can prevail. "Keep on sowing your seed," the Bible tells us (Eccles. 11:6). We can overcome the obstacles to soulfulness by rejecting easy and ready-made notions of manhood. We must concentrate on further development of our own unique versions of manhood. By keeping our own values at the center of our lives, we have a course to follow that is bound to lead to richness and personal wholeness. It is not just coincidence that such a course also brings us into greater harmony with God's plan for us.

For myself, I have tried to pinpoint the major tenets of my beliefs and share them through my writing. I think of my basic articles of faith as a kind of "personal Ten Commandments." What I have tried to do is create an extremely personal and masculine form for my values.

With the hope that what I have learned will benefit other men, my personal discoveries follow:

*The Ten Commandments of a Believing Man*

1. Love and appreciate your mother, yet make yourself available to a personal discovery of God and God's great nurturance.

2. Love and revere your father, yet free your heart to seek God, the everlasting Father.

3. Pursue the pathway of moral courage and learn to recognize it among fellow men and women.

4. Be truthful in all your words and deeds, and believe in the ultimate rewards that accompany authenticity.

5. Let faith be the fundamental experience in your life.

6. Work diligently, and work at what matters most in life.

7. Play with great zest for life, and allow play to live in harmony with the rest of your calling.

8. Do not partition the world; see it as a whole, full of majesty and life.

9. Choose a partner with spirituality in mind, and give of yourself freely and wholeheartedly to your spouse and children.

10. Love God with all your soul, and learn to accept that God loves you in kind.

These values provide me with a beacon with which to embrace the future. They help me to remember that my personal history is a part of God's plan, just as it is for every man.

The exploration of the male soul reveals that true comfort with manliness calls for the development of a spiritual world view. Manliness is fundamentally a soulful phenomenon. As such, it must include all aspects of a man—his spirit, mind, and body. Yet the development of a meaningful world view, and of faith itself, requires that a man be true to his own journey. In that journey a man encounters God and learns about the meaning of his life.

By the strength of God's will, and our own determination, we are renewed. We can then receive the greatest manhood of all, a sense of humanity conceived in the image of God. That is the soul of a man—the great destiny that awaits us.

# REFERENCES

Courtney, Alice, and Thomas Whipple. *Sex Stereotyping in Advertising.* Boston: D. C. Heath and Co., 1983.

Garfinkel, Perry. *In a Man's World.* New York: New American Library, 1985.

Greenspan, Bud. "Just a Few Feet Away." *Parade,* 10 March 1985, 4.

Heller, David. *The Children's God.* Chicago and London: The University of Chicago Press, 1986.

———. *Dear God: Children's Letters to God.* New York: Doubleday, 1987.

———. *Dear God: What Religion Were the Dinosaurs?* New York: Doubleday, 1990.

Hollander, Anne. "Dressed to Thrill." *The New Republic,* 28 January 1985, 28.

Küng, Hans. *Does God Exist?* New York: Vintage Books, 1981.

———. *Freud and the Problem of God.* New Haven: Yale University Press, 1979.

Pleck, Joseph, and Jack Sawyer, eds. *Men and Masculinity.* Englewood Cliffs, N.J.: Prentice-Hall, 1974.

Richmond, Peter. "Athletes and Drugs—A Growing Problem." *Knight-Ridder Newspapers,* 8 January 1985.

Smith, W. C. *The Meaning and End of Religion.* New York: New American Library, 1962.

# ABOUT THE AUTHOR

David Heller holds a Ph.D. from the University of Michigan and is a graduate of Harvard University. His other books include: *Dear God: What Religion Were the Dinosaurs?*, *Dear God: Children's Letters to God*, *The Pleasure of Psychology*, *The Children's God*, *Power in Psychotherapeutic Practice* and *Talking to Your Child About God*. His work has been featured in such periodicals as *USA Today*, *Good Housekeeping*, *Psychology Today*, *Parents Magazine*, *Redbook*, and *Catholic Digest*. David lives in Boston with his wife, Elizabeth.